Your Kitten's First Year

Shawn Messonnier, D.V.M.

Seaside Press

Library of Congress Cataloging-in-Publication Data

Messonnier, Shawn.
   Your kitten's first year / Shawn Messonnier.
      p.   cm.
   Includes index.
   ISBN 1-55622-527-X (PB)
   1. Kittens.   I. Title.
   SF447.M48   1996
   636.8'07--dc21   96-48154
                                             CIP

Seaside Press is an imprint of Wordware Publishing, Inc.
No part of this book may be reproduced in any form or by any means
without permission in writing from Wordware Publishing, Inc.

Printed in the United States of America

ISBN 1-55622-527-X
10 9 8 7 6 5 4 3 2 1
9611

All inquiries for volume purchases of this book should be addressed to
Wordware Publishing, Inc., at 1506 Capital Avenue, Plano, Texas 75074.
Telephone inquiries may be made by calling:

(972) 423-0090

Contents

Acknowledgments

A special thanks to my wonderful clients for their assistance with providing friendly kittens for photography. Thanks also to the folks at the Living Materials Center in Plano for their help with my last book, *Exotic Pets: A Veterinary Guide for Owners*. To the folks at Wordware Publishing, Inc., thanks for your faith in the message *Your Kitten's First Year* has to offer new kitten owners. Thanks always to my wife Sandy and daughter Erica for understanding my inattentiveness during deadlines. Your support means a lot.

Introduction

As a veterinarian, I am always thrilled when a pet owner brings in a kitten for its first visit. These owners are excited about their new pets, and it's exciting for me because I get to teach them how to properly care for their new family members. Raising a kitten can be fun, but at times it can also be challenging and frustrating. Sometimes owners, armed with incorrect information, have a difficult time raising the new kitten. Most don't have any idea what to expect from their new pet.

I believe that veterinarians should take time on the first visit or even before the first visit to properly discuss with the new or prospective owner exactly what to expect that important first year! A new kitten requires time, commitment, a lot of love and attention, and often a sizable financial investment.

No one should own a kitten without being fully prepared for this awesome responsibility. To help better prepare you for the trials and tribulations of kittenhood, I wrote *Your Kitten's First Year*. Unlike some kitten books, this book is written by a practicing veterinarian who deals with new kitten owners' questions and concerns on a daily basis. I've tried to cover as many topics as possible; ideas for what to include in the book have come from the numerous questions, comments, and suggestions often posed by new kitten owners. An important part of this book is the discussion concerning what it costs to raise a kitten and how to afford the care a new kitten requires. While this information might discourage some of you from owning a kitten, my intention is to better prepare you for those unexpected expenses that invariably arise after purchasing that new kitten.

Kittens are fun and playful and bring a smile to our faces. Enjoy your new kitten, and do a good job raising him. When you need advice, don't hesitate to turn to *Your Kitten's First Year* for answers.

Chapter 1

Choosing a Kitten

• •

Choosing a kitten seems easy enough. You just decide if you want a male or female, go to the local pet shop, spend several hundred dollars, and pick the cutest kitten in the window. You take it home, provide it nutrition, love, and regular veterinary care. It never gets sick and lives to a ripe old age. Ah, if only life were so easy.

Choosing a kitten is a difficult job. Unfortunately, so many people make an impulse buy based on emotion, only to find out the kitten is sick, has behavioral problems, or costs a lot in upkeep. These poor kittens, chosen on the spur of the moment, often end up euthanized before their third birthday. It is estimated that twelve to

twenty million dogs and cats are euthanized in animal shelters each year. Careful planning for a new kitten can prevent many of these needless deaths.

Pets are not disposable items. It takes time to evaluate your reasons for wanting a cat and then decide on the right one.

Ideally, you should choose and then visit with a veterinarian *before* purchasing a kitten. Veterinarians are trained to help you decide if a kitten is for you and can help you decide which breed may best suit you. Finally, the veterinarian can give you a realistic idea of the care and the expense involved in caring for this pet over the next ten to twenty years.

1

Why Do You Want a Kitten?

This is an extremely important question all potential kitten owners should ponder before bringing home their kitten. What are your reasons for wanting a kitten? Companionship? Status? A playmate for the kids?

What Breed to Choose?

Once again, a visit with your veterinarian can help you decide which breed may be best for you. What breed you pick is dependent upon several factors.

••➡ Many cat owners choose a mixed breed or alley cat. The technical terms for these cats are domestic short hair cat (DSH) or domestic long hair cat (DLH). These designations obviously have to do with the length of the cat's hair. Longer haired cats require frequent (daily) brushing to prevent mats from forming (mats commonly form on the underside of the cat). Longer haired cats often have more problems with hairballs as well (see Chapter 11: Congenital Medical Problems). There is no difference in behavior or disposition between a short or long haired cat.

••➡ Some cat owners prefer a specific pure breed of cat. Common breeds include Siamese, Persian, and Himalayan. As is true with dogs, pure breeds of cats are more prone to specific breed-associated medical problems than mixed breed cats. A visit with your veterinarian prior to purchasing a kitten will help you decide if a pure breed or mixed breed cat is best for you.

••➡ If you want a breed that doesn't shed very much, you might consider a Rex. Shedding can be controlled with daily brushing and a product called Prozyme (see Chapter 5: Feeding Your Kitten)

••➡ If you really want a male cat, a calico is not for you. True calico cats (tricolor cats) are females (although a rare male cat with XXY chromosomes does occasionally occur).

All purebred cats are prone to breed-specific problems. That's not to say that every member of that breed will develop a problem, only that cats of a particular breed have a higher chance of contracting a specific problem than the general cat population. As a rule, mixed breeds are usually sturdier and less likely to develop problems than purebred cats.

Kitten or Adult?

Okay, so you've decided a cat is definitely for you. After careful study and discussion with your veterinarian, you've even made a decision about which breed may best suit you. Now you have to decide if a young kitten or older cat is what you want.

A kitten can be a great companion for children.

Obviously, since this book is about kittens, most of you will choose a kitten over an older cat. However, while kittens can be fine pets, so too can older cats. Remember that kittens require a lot of work and expense their first year. If you don't have the time or don't want to go to the trouble and expense of kitten care, you should seriously consider adopting an older pet, especially one that may be at the local pound. Some of these cats are purebred pets (although without registration papers), and most if not all of them will make excellent pets.

An older cat may require less care.

Here are some points to ponder when deciding between a young kitten or older cat.

•• ➡ Kittens must have a series of vaccinations, dewormings, and spaying or neutering; many older pets have already had these procedures performed.

•• ➡ Kittens like to scratch and bite during their play activity; most older cats do not have these problems.

•• ➡ Most kittens have not had time to develop behavioral problems; some older cats may have behavioral problems.

••➡ You can train your kitten the way you want; you and you alone will determine what kind of pet it will become. Older cats have already been trained by another owner. They may have been left at the pound because the owner mistrained the kitten and now it is an older cat with behavioral problems that its former owner could not handle.

••➡ Many kittens have medical problems including worms (parasites), fleas, ear mites, or respiratory infections; most older cats are healthy (although they may harbor intestinal parasites and should be checked for this condition).

••➡ Some kittens may have congenital conditions that may not be apparent until they get a little older; older cats have usually had time to show any signs of congenital diseases.

••➡ Kittens are fun and playful; it is a joy to watch them explore and learn about their environment; older cats have already experienced this energetic time of "kittenhood."

While it may appear that the odds are stacked in favor of purchasing an older cat, that's not really true. There are positive and negative benefits about owning either a kitten or older cat. As a prospective owner, you need to make an informed decision. If you can handle all the challenges of kittenhood, you will be rewarded with much happiness watching that kitten grow and mature and live a long, healthy life.

TEETHING ....

Kittens go through a "teething" phase, just like children. Until six months of age, when most or all of the adult teeth have erupted, your kitten will gradually lose his baby teeth. Unlike the case with children, the procedure is usually not painful and often goes unnoticed. Kittens usually do not act irritable, get diarrhea, or develop a fever as new teeth erupt. However, teething kittens usually need to chew on something. You can help them out by offering a variety of chew toys as suggested by your veterinarian.

MONTHLY PET HEALTH
CHECKLIST

New kittens owners are often overly concerned about their kitten's health. An occasional cough or sneeze, one mild bout of vomiting or diarrhea, and an occasional itch are not usually cause for concern. Your kitten is not that different from you. Since you wouldn't call the doctor if you coughed a few times, there is no reason to panic if your kitten also exhibits an occasional mild symptom. There are times when you should be concerned. Persistent vomiting, diarrhea, coughing, sneezing, itching, or lack of appetite or energy are reasons to call the doctor. The following home health checklist, which should be used monthly, can help you decide if your kitten requires veterinary attention.

Answer "yes" or "no" to the following questions. Call your doctor if you answer "yes" to any of the questions.

My kitten. . . .
walks with pain or difficulty.
has abnormal stool.
urinates abnormally.
has an abnormal appetite; eats or drinks too much or too little.
vomits.
has difficulty breathing.
has offensive breath odor.
does not have clean white teeth and pink healthy gums.
has lumps or bumps on his body.
has ticks or fleas or ear mites.
shakes his head.
licks, chews, bites at, or scratches himself constantly.
passes out or tires easily.
has discharge from the eyes, nose, mouth, anus, or genitals.

Common Owner Concerns

• •

Q: I have several small children and we are considering purchasing a kitten for them. Are there any breeds I should avoid? We certainly don't want to pick a kitten that will be aggressive and bite or scratch the children as it gets older.

A: There is no one breed that is best for every situation. However, there are some generalities which should be considered:

If you can see both the mother and father of the kittens, and they are friendly and outgoing, especially around children, your kitten will most likely inherit these desirable behaviors as well. How a kitten turns out depends quite a bit on genetics but also on the way you raise it. For this reason, it's critical that owners get the proper instructions on behavior management from their doctors. Families with children may want to avoid purchasing an older cat (unless the cat is familiar and known to enjoy children) since there is no way to tell if the older cat was socialized with children and how the previous owners raised it.

To prevent cat bites, kittens should be disciplined for biting, biting games should be discouraged, and all people in the house should be taught the proper methods of reward and punishment. All house members should discipline the kitten for unacceptable behaviors. Kittens should be neutered or spayed to prevent hormone-induced aggression. Kittens should be trained so that all family members can remove food or toys from the kitten without it showing signs of aggression. Small children should be trained not to approach cats without a parent assisting (many bites are precipitated when the child approaches a cat, even a friend's cat, and displays what the cat considers a threatening gesture, as when the child may grab for the cat, its food, or toys.) Finally, to prevent possible problems, infants and toddlers should never be left alone with a cat (although cats will not suck the breath out of a child).

Behavior problems, especially those involving aggression, are best prevented.

Q: Where should I acquire a kitten? Is one source better than another?

A: Ideally, if you can see the mother and father of the kittens in person, this is a great situation. If the parent cats exhibit any undesirable behaviors, such as aggression or excessive timidity, this can be observed. If the parents have any medical or physical characteristics which might be passed to the kittens, this may also be determined. If both parents seem in excellent health and physical shape and do not exhibit any undesirable behaviors, you can be reasonably certain the kittens will also be of the same high quality.

While many people feel that pet stores are the worst places to buy kittens, a recent study failed to reveal a significant increase of illness in puppies from pet stores. The information is probably relevant to kittens as well. Here's some of what the study, as reported in the June 15, 1994 issue of the *Journal of the American Veterinary Medical Association,* had to say:

1. The risk of acquiring a fatally ill puppy is low regardless of where it is acquired (breeder, pet store, humane society).

VACATION FOR YOUR KITTEN ....

While you're away on vacation, your kitten can "vacation" at your veterinarian's hospital in the boarding area (kennel). Some owners are concerned about how their pet will fare while they are away. Most pets do well during their boarding visit. Prior to boarding your pet, make sure it's current on all its vaccinations. It's also a good idea for you to see the kennel and make sure you are comfortable with it. Ask about ventilation and heating and air-conditioning. Find out how often pets are handled, what brand of food is fed and how often, and what happens in case of an emergency.

While many owners like to leave a favorite toy or bedding with the kitten, many facilities discourage this practice. While it doesn't happen often, a boarding pet could destroy a toy and swallow a piece which might cause an injury. For this reason, it's safer not to leave anything for the kitten. Most boarding kittens don't even play with any of the toys that owners leave for them. While it may make you feel better, the kitten does fine without the toys.

2. The risk of respiratory disease is higher for puppies obtained from pet stores, but serious disease is rare and doesn't differ significantly between sources. The stress of weaning, shipping, handling, and exposure to other puppies increases the risk of respiratory disease.

3. Puppies from humane societies had the second highest incidence of respiratory disease, followed by those acquired from breeders and finally private owners.

4. Regardless of source, puppies 10-12 weeks old had the highest risk of respiratory disease.

5. Puppies from humane societies and pet stores had the highest incidence of intestinal disease; severe disease was rare regardless of source of acquisition. As with respiratory disease, stresses associated with weaning, shipping, handling, and mixing puppies contributed to intestinal disease.

6. Puppies purchased from private owners had the highest incidence of roundworms, a disease that can be fatal in puppies and kittens if not detected and treated early. This disease can also be contracted from puppies and kittens by owners.

7. Puppies acquired from pet stores had a low prevalence of intestinal parasites due to routine deworming programs.

8. Flea control was better in pet stores puppies than those bought from private owners or the humane societies.

9. Puppies from breeders and pet stores had a higher incidence of ear mites.

10. Approximately 7-15 percent of puppies have some type of congenital defects.

These findings indicate that regardless of source, the risk of death or serious illness was low. There is no ideal source from which to acquire a kitten. Certainly, observing and interacting with the parents of the kitten and its littermates gives the prospective buyer a chance to check for problems that might affect the kitten; this is obviously not possible if the kitten is purchased from a pet store (in many cases, *nothing* is known about the kitten's parents or littermates). The decision is up to the individual owner after considering all factors. Obviously, if you are not impressed with the seller or the facilities or quality of kittens, you should not try to be a "Good Samaritan" and purchase a kitten from that source. Kittens that are ill and which require veterinary care can be expensive to treat and may die anyway depending upon the type of disease present.

While it is ideal to be able to see the parents of the kitten, it is not essential for picking a happy, healthy kitten. Make sure the kitten is friendly, outgoing, and seems physically fit. Regardless of where you purchase the kitten, insist on a guarantee in your written contract that allows you to return the kitten if a veterinarian finds any major health problems; have the kitten examined as soon after purchase as possible, ideally within 24 to 48 hours.

CLEAN TEETH MEAN A HEALTHY BODY . . . .

Dental disease is the #1 disease of cats three years of age and older. One thing you can do at home that will decrease the number of visits (and the cost!) for professional cleaning (which is usually needed on average once a year) is *daily* brushing of your kitten's teeth. All you need is a soft-bristled child's toothbrush and some water. Spend only about 5-10 seconds several times each day and gently brush the outside surfaces of the teeth (it's almost impossible to get any pet to let you brush the inner surfaces). Brush as you would your own teeth. Avoid human toothpaste or baking soda and hydrogen peroxide as they can foam up in the pet's mouth and make the experience unpleasant. Most kittens think of the brushing as a game and easily accept it. Training your kitten to accept tooth brushing not only controls dental disease but trains him to allow you to do an important procedure without a struggle.

Chapter 2
Choosing
Your Kitten's Doctor

• •

Choosing a veterinarian is an extremely important job for pet owners. As with choosing the family doctor or dentist, choosing a veterinarian for the new kitten shouldn't be left to chance or done on a whim. Remember, this person will most likely be providing health care for your four-legged family member for many years. You need to choose someone you trust, someone you can develop a rapport with, someone who shares the same health care philosophy with you, and someone who is convenient and offers high-quality, affordable care.

Ideally, the time to choose a veterinarian is *before* you ever purchase your kitten. Your veterinarian can help you make the right choice in a pet. Maybe a kitten isn't for you; possibly some other pet would be a better match for your situation. If a kitten is the way to go, which breed should you choose? While most pet owners will acquire a domestic short hair (DSH) or domestic long hair (DLH), some owners may wish to have a more expensive purebred kitten, such as a Persian or Siamese, as a pet. Your veterinarian can give you advice on proper selection of a kitten after carefully consulting with you and your family and finding out your interests.

You should plan on taking your new kitten to the doctor very soon after purchasing it, ideally the same day. Most sellers, including pet stores and

11

breeders, give owners five to seven days to have their kitten examined. Some sellers stipulate that the kitten must be examined within 48 hours of purchase. If the kitten isn't examined within the stipulated time frame, the buyer's contract and health guarantee is voided. This means that if the kitten isn't examined within the stated time after purchase, the treatment of any problems or diseases detected by the doctor are the owner's responsibility. Within the terms of the contract, an owner whose kitten is found to have a problem within the stated time frame will be compensated by the seller. Let's say for example that you take your kitten to the veterinarian the day it is purchased. During the initial exam, the doctor discovers a coccidial intestinal infection, a relatively common problem in new kittens. Diagnosis and treatment for coccidiosis might be $30-$40. Because the kitten was examined while it was still "under warranty," you are reimbursed in full by the seller. Had you waited a week or more, you would not be reimbursed for the cost of the treatment.

Of course this is just an example, and every seller will have different conditions in the

warranty (make sure you ask for and receive a warranty or written contract with your new kitten!). The point is that once the kitten is purchased, you don't have time to visit several veterinarians and try to choose the right one for you. You must be comfortable with your decision; spend the time looking around *before* you buy the kitten.

Choosing a doctor for your pet is serious business, and it's a task that should not be taken lightly. Ask friends or family members to recommend a veterinarian, or call the local veterinary association (the phone number is usually available in the yellow pages under the "veterinary" listing). After compiling a list of prospective or possible veterinarians, it's time to do some investigating. If you follow the procedures listed below, you should have no problem narrowing your selection to that one "perfect" veterinarian.

●●➡ **Call the office and ask questions.** You want to find out how the staff treats you on the phone. A rude or uncaring attitude is an indication of how you'll be treated in the office. Since you'll be doing most of your business with the staff and not the doctor, it's imperative that you are satisfied with them. Of course, everyone can have a bad day at one time or another. So if you are treated rudely on the phone, you may want to try a second call, or choose another veterinarian from your remaining list of names.

Some questions to ask during your telephone inquiry:

1. What vaccinations and other services does my kitten need?
2. What is the cost for those services?
3. What are the office hours?
4. What forms of payment are accepted?
5. Are clients billed? (To keep costs down, most veterinarians don't bill.)
6. Does the veterinarian take emergency calls? (Most don't.)

The answers to these questions, are not as important as *how* they are answered. A staff member who can't comfortably answer these questions might be indicative of an overall problem (poorly trained staff) at the office. Make sure you're com-

AFTER HOURS VETERINARY CARE ....

Most veterinarians do not take emergency calls. However, pets often get sick after hours and require immediate care. Many cities have animal emergency clinics for after-hours treatment.

While emergency clinics can literally be life-savers, you need to be aware of several things. First, because they are emergency clinics, you should avoid using them for routine problems; go instead to your regular veterinarian. Second, because of the overhead cost, expect to pay more for this specialized care. Third, because they offer strictly temporary care, you will probably still need to go to your regular veterinarian the next day.

If you're not sure if you have a true emergency, call the clinic and ask their advice. If you need to go, call ahead so the staff can give you instructions and prepare for your arrival. Ask your own doctor the name, address, and phone number of the emergency clinic he uses and keep the number handy. Finally, don't put off minor problems until they become big problems (usually on the weekends or holidays) that require emergency care.

fortable with how you are treated on the phone.

•• ➡ **Visit the office.** If you're happy with the way you have been treated on the phone, ask to visit the office. Any office should allow you to stop by for a quick tour and possible introduction to the doctor. An office that refuses a tour may have something to hide: *beware!* Realize that certain times may be busy or inconvenient for the staff, so work with them to arrange a mutually satisfactory time.

•• ➡ **Look, listen, and, most importantly, smell.** Is the parking area clean, safe, and close to the office? You don't want to have to walk far with a pet that might get loose or expose your pet to unsafe conditions. Does the office appear and smell clean? While occasional "accidents" on the floor do occur, a dirty or smelly office might indicate that the place is not kept clean and sanitary, certainly not a place you want your pet to visit. Is the staff warm and courteous in person as well as on the phone? Do you get to see everything, including the boarding area, surgical facilities, and treatment rooms? If you don't feel comfortable in the office,

neither will your pet; look elsewhere.

•• ➡ **Meet the doctor.** Most doctors will be glad to meet a prospective client for a few minutes at no charge. Don't be afraid to ask the doctor any questions you have, such as:

1. Where and when did you receive your degree?

2. How long have you been in practice?

3. Do you have any specialized interests (birds, dermatology, surgery, etc.)?

4. Do you treat clients with after-hours emergencies or refer them to a reputable facility?

5. Do you have any pets of your own?

6. When is your day off, and who fills in when you are gone?

7. Do you feel pets should be spayed or neutered, and at what age?

As you question the doctor, notice *how* the questions are answered. You should feel comfortable with the doctor and the staff. Remember, you will be entrusting your pet's care to this person for possibly 15-20 years.

•• ➡ **Price ... Quality ... Service. Pick any two.** I've heard this saying many times, and it's so true. If you want a low price, you usually have to give up high quality or superior service. As you make calls to schedule visits with the various offices, you'll probably find a wide range of answers to questions about the price of services. For example, some veterinarians may charge $50 for the first kitten visit, whereas others charge $20. Some doctors may charge $120 to spay a pet; another doctor might quote you $30! What's going on here? Are you being ripped off?

Probably not; the difference in price is related to the difference in the quality of care and

---

MALPRACTICE ....

Most veterinarians don't have the malpractice worries that "people doctors" face on a daily basis. However, since anyone can file a lawsuit, no matter how frivolous, at any time, veterinarians must always strive to prevent problems from occurring.

By definition, malpractice must involve an action that a veterinarian takes (or fails to take) that another veterinarian of reasonable judgement would not have taken (or would have taken if needed) that results in measurable harm or death to the patient.

As an example, if your healthy kitten dies after a spaying procedure, is that malpractice? It all depends. Assuming the doctor performed the surgery as another doctor of similar skill would have, even though the kitten died there was no malpractice. However, if that doctor administered the incorrect dose of anesthetic, this would possibly be malpractice.

Let's suppose that a doctor accidentally left a surgical sponge in your kitten's abdomen after a spay. Even though that is negligent and not normal procedure, unless your kitten suffered from it (developed an infection or died as a direct result of the sponge), no malpractice was committed since no harm was done.

Remember, for malpractice to occur there must be a negligent action or inaction *and* measurable harm must occur as a direct result of the negligent act.

the level of customer service you receive.

For example, the average new kitten visit at my office takes 30-60 minutes. We feel justified in charging a higher price for the time we will take, thoroughly examining the pet, teaching the owner how to be a responsible kitten owner, explaining diet and training, laying the foundation for a life

of proper health care, and answering questions. Lower-cost facilities may rush clients in and out in an effort to see as many as possible. Make sure your veterinarian administers only the best vaccinations, always using a new needle and syringe (some places actually give vaccinations with used, but supposedly "resterilized," needles and syringes).

Common Owner Concerns...

Word-of-Mouth Referrals

Q: My next door neighbor raved about her veterinarian. Is he the one I should choose for my new kitten?

A: From the doctor's viewpoint, clients who choose them because of word-of-mouth referrals are often their best clients. If one client is satisfied, he or she will likely refer friends. These new clients are usually also outstanding clients.

While getting suggestions from friends is a great way to gather a few names for your list, it is still necessary to actually do some investigative work on your own. Just because your friend

likes a certain doctor and his policies doesn't mean that you will. Think of friends as a great starting place for names to add to your list of prospective doctors.

Choosing a Doctor from the Phone Book

Q: The yellow pages seem like a convenient way to find a doctor. Is there anything I should worry about when choosing a doctor from the phone book?

A: While the yellow pages are used by people for many things, most people don't choose a doctor from this source. The research I did for a marketing book for veterinarians showed that, on average, only about 7 percent of new clients came from the yellow pages. The yellow pages can be helpful to select a few doctors in a certain location, however. Let's say that you don't want to go more than five miles from your home for a veterinarian. Using the phone book, you can pick out veterinary offices near you to add to your list of prospective veterinarians.

One note of caution: Don't believe everything you read! Realize that as with any source of advertising, ads in the phone book are meant to attract your attention and get you to respond. Not everything in an ad is necessarily true and accurate. For example, some doctors advertise that they treat birds. While they may offer treatment for birds, it doesn't necessarily mean they know what they are doing! Use the ads as a source, but don't be over-impressed with what you read. If something sounds too good to be true, it usually is!

Driving in the Neighborhood

Q: I pass several clinics driving to work each day. They all are convenient for me. How do I decide which one is best?

A: Many people choose a veterinarian because they have seen the office and its location is convenient. That's not the best way to choose a veterinarian, but it is helpful in compiling your list of possible choices. The only way you can ultimately decide which doctor is best for your pet is by calling and then visiting the office. After some investigative work, you will be able to decide which doctor best suits your needs.

Differences in Costs

Q: I've called several offices and it seems like there is quite a range in the costs for vaccinations. Why do some doctors charge more than others for the same shots?

A: In the competitive environment in which we live, it's no surprise that discount pet clinics have appeared on the scene. In order to hook you as a client, a clinic may offer cut-rate prices (and corresponding cut-rate care) to lure you in. As a client, you and you alone have to make a choice regarding the care for your new kitten. Do you want high-quality care or low-cost care? There is no right or wrong, only choices—choices you make and you will have to live with once you make your decision.

Hospital or Clinic

Q: Some veterinary offices are called "hospitals" whereas others are called "clinics." What's the difference?

A: Often, very little. As of this writing, veterinarians can choose whatever names they want for their offices. The terms "hospital" and "clinic" are interchangeable. Many doctors feel that the term "hospital" sounds more professional than "clinic," and some hospitals do offer more services than clinics offer. In the end, the name probably has more to do with the veterinarian's self-esteem and self-image than with anything else. Most veterinarians probably choose the term "hospital" because it

---

AN OWNER'S RESPONSIBILITY . . . .

Neither in human nor veterinary medicine can a guaranteed cure ever be offered. While we can always do our best to cure a problem, there are too many factors involved that doctors can't control to ever promise a certain outcome. What if the outcome is not as expected? What if your pet dies during what should be a "routine" procedure? What is your responsibility?

You may be surprised to discover that legally you are required to pay for all requested services regardless of the outcome. Let's suppose that your "normal" kitten dies after what seemed to be a routine spay surgery. Are you still responsible for payment? Yes. The reason is because no guarantee as to the outcome of the procedure was given. You requested a spay, and even though the surgery resulted in the unfortunate death of your kitten, you are still responsible for payment for the services you requested.

No doctor can ever guarantee any treatment or surgery, and no procedure or surgery should ever be considered "routine." While extremely uncommon, there are rare instances of normal-appearing pets dying during or after properly performed medical and surgical procedures. Know the risks of the procedure before making the decision to schedule the surgery.

implies high quality care; the term "clinic" implies a lower quality level of care.

Is Low Cost Really Worth It?

Q: Why do some doctors offer low-cost neutering and spaying, whereas others charge two to three times as much?

A: Regarding spays and neuters, the higher price usually includes additional services, such as a pre-surgical examination and blood tests to make sure it's safe to anesthetize your pet. For example, after the exam and blood tests the veterinarian may then sedate the animal, which reduces the amount of anesthetic needed, making the procedure safer. The veterinarian may use isoflurane, a very expensive anesthetic gas, but also the safest. A more expensive suture material may be used for the stitches which helps reduce infection and swelling after the surgery, and your pet may be monitored during the surgery by an assistant as well as various machines. Post-operative care is also a factor.

Consequently you may be cutting the quality of your pet's care by cutting costs. You as the owner must decide if cost or quality will be the driving factor in choosing a veterinarian for your pet. For tips on cutting costs without sacrificing care, see Chapter 13: Lowering the Cost of Pet Care.

GETTING A SECOND OPINION ....

Most pet owners are happy with their doctors. Unless a problem
arises, a pet owner has little reason to seek the opinion of another
veterinarian. But what if you're not happy with your doctor? What
if, despite his best recommendations, your kitten continues to be
sick and not improve? What can you do?

Before you jump ship, consider asking your veterinarian *why*
he thinks the problem isn't getting better. Could the diagnosis or
treatment be incorrect? Could your pet be one of those rare ones
that doesn't respond to the "usual" treatment for the disease?

Be honest with yourself as well. Do you have anything to do
with your pet not improving? For example, are you giving your
pet the medicine exactly as prescribed by the doctor? So often the
reason for a pet not getting better or getting better and then relaps-
ing is that the owner is not giving all of the medication as
prescribed. Have you placed any financial constraints on the doctor? If you declined any tests that may be necessary to accurately
diagnose and treat your pet, chances are your pet may never get
better! The more information you give your doctor (by agreeing to
his recommendations for diagnostic testing and treatment), the
greater the chance for a correct diagnosis and treatment.

If you still feel a second opinion is needed, there's nothing
wrong with that. You can assist the new doctor if you bring copies
of your previous medical records. I suggest a second opinion if
your pet has had a chronic problem for several months and is not
improving despite the fact that your regular doctor has tried
several different treatments and you have not placed financial
constraints on him. Getting a second opinion will, as a rule, cost
more than a first opinion. Be prepared to agree to extensive diagnostic testing in order for the new doctor to give you an honest
and valuable second opinion.

THE MEDICAL TRIANGLE ....

What determines if your kitten will recover if she becomes ill? There are three things that determine a kitten's chance for a successful outcome, and these three things make up what is often referred to as the medical triangle. The three things are you, the doctor, and the pet.

You . . . As owner, you have a say in whether or not your kitten has a good chance of recovering from an illness. If you take your kitten to the doctor when she first becomes ill, rather than wait a few days, her chances of recovery are greater. How much you spend on health care for your kitten also affects her chances of recovery. If your doctor recommends blood tests, radiographs, and hospitalization, and you decline these recommendations due to cost, your kitten has less chance for fully recovering quickly than if you followed the doctor's recommendations. Finally, you must administer medications to your kitten as directed. If you are unable to give pills or liquid medications to your kitten, she may not recover. Also, if you stop giving the medications too soon (a common problem), your kitten might temporarily recover but then relapse and become more seriously ill.

Your doctor . . . Your choice of doctors also affect you kitten's chances for a successful recovery. If your doctor is committed to continuing education and keeps up with the latest medical developments, this improves your kitten's chances for a successful diagnosis and recovery. If your doctor believes in preventive care, this will decrease your costs of care as your kitten is less likely to become ill. If your doctor recommends the best care for your kitten, this will improve her chance for recovery.

Your kitten . . . Finally, your kitten ultimately determines her chances for recovery. No matter how good a job your doctor does diagnosing her condition and prescribing the correct course of therapy, and no matter how good you are in following the doctor's recommendations, ultimately how strong your kitten is determines whether or not she will recover. If her immune system is strong, she has a greater chance of recovery than if she has a weak immune system.

Chapter 3
Vaccinations

. . . .

An important part of health care for your kitten is a series of shots, or vaccinations. These vaccinations occur in a series that will be repeated throughout the life of the pet.

Vaccinations are an inexpensive way to protect your pet from the common diseases that are easily transmitted between other cats and your pet.

There are several reasons to have your pet properly immunized:

••➡ Regular vaccinations are the least expensive way to prevent common diseases.

••➡ Vaccinations are the only way to prevent certain fatal diseases.

••➡ Vaccinations are required before your kitten can be boarded, groomed, or hospitalized.

••➡ Having your pet vaccinated demonstrates your responsibility as a loving, caring pet owner.

Most of the time, you will choose to have your kitten vaccinated at your regular veterinarian's office. There are two other options that you may hear about, however. Both of these options are inferior to visiting your regular doctor and can jeopardize not only your pet's health but its life and your health as well.

Vaccination Clinics. Mobile, parking-lot shot clinics are a common sight in many communities. At these clinics, low-cost vaccinations are given in a conveyor-belt fashion. While these shots do usually cost less than those at your regular doctor's, *buyer beware!* There are many negative aspects about these clinics:

1. While they charge less than a full-service hospital, they don't charge that much less (usually $5-$10 less at most).

2. You may pay less, but you also get less. The cost of the vaccination probably does not include a fecal exam for parasites or a thorough physical exam. While vaccinations are extremely important, the exam is even more important. Why? Think about it: how many pets do you personally know that have died from rabies or distemper? Very few if any. Yet, how many pets die each year of kidney, liver, or heart failure, or cancer? Many. The only way to accurately diagnose these common conditions is with a yearly examination and appropriate laboratory tests. While vaccinations are important, so is the physical examination; don't put your pet's health at risk just to save a few dollars.

3. At low-cost shot clinics, your kitten is not an individual but rather a number. Maintaining a regular relationship with one

doctor is important in establishing continuity of care.

4. At the low-cost clinics, your kitten will be exposed to all the other pets standing in line, waiting for the shots. You have no way of knowing if any of these other pets are current on their vaccinations. More than likely they are not; many have never had any vaccinations (some studies have found that up to half of the pets at the "shot clinics" do not receive regular veterinary care!). By taking your kitten to its regular doctor, you will limit its exposure to unvaccinated animals.

5. Vaccinations are required for boarding, grooming, and showing your pet. Some facilities will not accept vaccinations done at low-cost clinics, due to the questionable practices at some of these places. This means you'll have to pay for your pet to be revaccinated; while revaccination will not harm your pet, it is an unnecessary expense you can prevent.

Do-It-Yourself Vaccinations.
Some pharmacies and pet supply catalogs sell over-the-counter vaccine kits for you to administer the vaccinations yourself. As with low-cost clinics, there are problems with this practice.

1. As mentioned above, vaccinations are required for boarding, grooming, and showing your pet. Most facilities will not accept vaccinations done at home, as there is no proof that the vaccinations were done correctly or even done at all! This means you'll have to pay for your pet to be revaccinated, resulting in an unnecessary expense.

2. Vaccinations require special handling and need constant refrigeration. If you purchase vaccines at a grocery store pharmacy, how do you know they were refrigerated promptly upon arrival and not kept on the hot loading dock all day? Did you promptly refrigerate the vaccines after purchase, or did they spend a few hours on the hot dashboard of your car while you ran other errands?

3. What if you accidentally vaccinate yourself while attempting to vaccinate your cat? This happens frequently; while you won't catch any of the diseases contained within the vaccine, you can develop a nasty, infected abscess.

4. What if your kitten jumps at the wrong time and you only get half the vaccine in him, squirting the rest into the air?

Should you revaccinate him, or is half a vaccine good enough?

5. Vaccinating at home means your kitten won't receive that very important annual examination and fecal test. While you can bring your kitten to the doctor just for these two things, you won't save any money doing this and may spend even more (most doctors price the vaccinations as a package; if you only need part of the package, such as the exam and fecal test, you still pay full price).

6. What if your pet develops a vaccine reaction after receiving its immunization? Can you get your kitten to the doctor in enough time for proper treatment? While most reactions are not life-threatening, some are; prompt treatment is needed.

7. While we never expect our own pets to bite us, it can happen. Giving a shot can be painful. What if your cat bites you as a result of the painful injection?

8. You can't legally give a rabies injection; only a licensed veterinarian can do that. This means you will still have to see your doctor for that. Most veterinarians charge a full office call in addition to the rabies injection, meaning you'll save no

money asking for just the rabies vaccine.

Your kitten will need a series of vaccinations until it is about four months old. The specific vaccinations that are needed are discussed below. These will vary from doctor to doctor; for now, it's important to understand what vaccines do, what they don't do, and why your new kitten needs so many.

Two Months Old (8 Weeks)

First veterinary visit (although this can also occur at 6 weeks of age if you acquire the kitten then):

• • ➡ Complete physical examination

• • ➡ First kitten vaccinations: Feline Viral Rhinotracheitis-Calici Virus-Panleukopenia-Chlamydia (FVRCP) (Note: Not all doctors offer the chlamydia vaccine; however, since it is a cause of respiratory disease in kittens, you should strongly consider it for your kitten)

• • ➡ Fecal exam for intestinal parasites

• • ➡ Heartworm preventive medication may be started on the kitten's first visit, depending upon the area of the country you live in and if the kitten will be an

---

WHEN TO VACCINATE FOR FELINE INFECTIOUS PERITONITIS (FIP). . . . .

An old disease and a new vaccine have prompted a lot of questions from pet owners. Feline infectious peritonitis, also called FIP, is a viral disease that has its highest incidence in young male outdoor cats. The disease can occur in two forms. In the classic form, fluid builds up in the cat's abdomen (peritonitis) and/or chest cavities. This is the most common presentation in the younger male cats. In about half of the infected cats (usually the older ones), the virus causes granulomas (chronic abscesses) anywhere in the cat's body. Signs that a cat has this dry form of FIP may depend upon what organ system is affected. Cats with the nervous system form may become blind, have seizures, or become paralyzed. Cats with the granulomas in their intestinal systems may have vomiting, diarrhea, or chronic wasting. Cats with the viral particles in the liver or kidneys may have chronic liver or

outdoor pet. I personally recommend keeping pets indoors to decrease the chance of illness, injury, or fatalities. Heartworm disease, while it can occur in cats, occurs much less often than in dogs. Prescribing heartworm preventive medication is controversial; the medicine, while safe to use in cats as prescribed by your veterinarian, is not approved for use in cats. Check with your doctor to see if your cat would benefit from heartworm preventive medication.

Three Months Old (12 Weeks)

Second veterinary visit:

••➡ Complete physical examination

••➡ Second kitten vaccinations: Feline Viral Rhinotracheitis-

Calici Virus-Panleukopenia-Chlamydia (FVRCP) (Note: Not all veterinarians vaccinate against the respiratory infection caused by the chlamydia organism.)

••➡ Feline Leukemia/Feline Immunodeficiency Virus (FIV) Test

••➡ First Feline Leukemia Vaccination

The leukemia/FIV test determines if your young kitten is infected with either of these fatal viruses. If the tests are negative, your kitten can receive its leukemia vaccination (there is not currently a vaccine for FIV, or feline AIDS infection). Kittens that test positive on either test should be retested in four to eight weeks. If the second test is negative, either the kitten eliminated the virus, the first test gave

kidney disease. This dry form is very difficult to diagnose in the living cat without a surgical biopsy; blood tests may suggest the disease but are not 100 percent accurate.

Recently an intranasal nose drop vaccine was developed. Previous attempts at injectable vaccines actually caused the disease in vaccinated cats. This new intranasal vaccine has avoided that problem, although one early study which has not been duplicated did find a higher incidence of FIP in vaccinated cats as compared with unvaccinated cats. FIP is a disease affecting mainly outdoor cats and multi-cat households. Discuss with your veterinarian your cat's need for this vaccine.

a "false-positive" reaction, or the virus is "hidden" in the kitten's body and will cause problems later. If the second series of tests is negative, the kitten can be vaccinated against leukemia.

Some doctors recommend vaccinating against feline infectious peritonitis (FIP), a contagious fatal disease which usually affects young outdoor cats. Because this vaccine is new and the subject of some controversy, not all doctors recommend it. You should discuss FIP with your doctor if you have any questions.

Four Months Old (16 Weeks)
Third veterinary visit:
• •➡ Complete physical examination
• •➡ Third kitten vaccinations: Feline Viral Rhinotracheitis-Calici Virus-Panleukopenia-Chlamydia (FVRCP) (Note: Not all veterinarians vaccinate against the respiratory infection caused by the chlamydia organism)
• •➡ Second Feline Leukemia Vaccination
• •➡ Rabies Vaccination (this may be given during the second visit depending upon local laws)
• •➡ Fecal exam for intestinal parasites

What Vaccines Do. . .
When your kitten receives an injection, it receives either a killed bacteria or virus or a modified live virus. These bacterium and viruses are killed or modified in such a way that they will stimulate the kitten's immune system to produce antibodies but not harm the kitten. Think of a vaccine as a source of foreign protein. When this foreign protein, called an antigen, is introduced into your kitten's body, the body will make antibodies against that protein (certain types of white blood cells will also be stimulated to provide a so-called "cell-mediated" immunity; however, to keep things simple, we'll just concentrate on the antibodies). These antibodies will protect the kitten the next time that foreign protein enters the body, as when the kitten might be exposed to the actual disease. These antibodies will protect the kitten from the disease. An unvaccinated kitten will also make antibodies against the disease, but the disease may kill the kitten before the antibodies have a chance to work. Pets are vaccinated annually to restimulate the body to produce more antibodies, as the antibodies don't last forever.

What Vaccines Don't Do...

No vaccine is perfect. A vaccine depends upon several things in order to work. The kitten must be capable of mounting an immune response and forming antibodies. While this is not a problem for most kittens, there are several times when a kitten may not be able to make antibodies. If the kitten doesn't make antibodies, the vaccine won't work.

1. A kitten won't make antibodies effectively if it's sick. Therefore, it's critical that a thorough examination be performed prior to vaccinating the kitten. Sick kittens should not be vaccinated.

2. A kitten can't make antibodies if it received antibodies from its mother that have not "worn off" yet. Assuming the mother cat is vaccinated, these "maternal" antibodies pass to the kitten after birth during nursing (specifically in the first one to two days after birth when the kitten consumes the colostrum, or antibody-rich milk). These antibodies offer short-term (usually several weeks to several months) protection against diseases. If a kitten is vaccinated while these maternal antibodies are still present, it will not make any antibodies of its

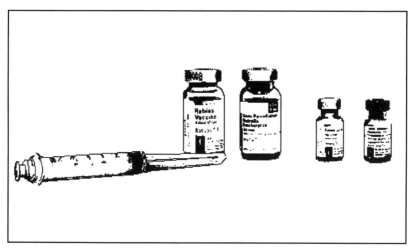

Vaccines protect your kitten from a variety of diseases.

own (see page 32 for further discussion of maternal antibodies and how they affect vaccinations).

3. Rarely, a kitten may be born with a deficient immune system and be incapable of making protective antibodies.

These kittens usually die within a few days after birth.

Assuming your kitten is capable of making protective antibodies, vaccinations will stimulate its immune system to make protective antibodies.

DON'T DO IT YOURSELF!! . . . .

In an attempt to save a few dollars, a few owners vaccinate their pets themselves. Vaccines are inexpensive and can be purchased from many pharmacies or pet supply catalogs. While this may seem like a great way to save on doctor bills, owners should seriously reconsider vaccinating pets themselves. Consider all that could go wrong with at-home vaccinations:

••➡ The vaccine may not be handled correctly. Did the pharmacy promptly refrigerate the vaccine, or was it left on the loading dock in the hot sun all day? Did you store it promptly and properly after purchase, or did you leave it on your hot car dashboard while you ran a few errands? Improperly storing vaccines can cause them to become inactive and useless.

••➡ The vaccine must be given correctly. The instructions and diagrams that accompany the vaccines are often hard to understand and in some cases inaccurate. Improperly giving a vaccine means the vaccine won't work.

••➡ Even though most owners don't think their pet would ever bite them, getting a shot hurts! You put yourself at risk if the pain from the injection causes your pet to unexpectedly bite you!

••➡ Vaccine manufacturers receive many reports each year from owners who accidentally vaccinate themselves. While you won't catch the disease you're vaccinating for, you can get a nasty, infected wound.

Despite what many people think, no vaccine is 100 percent effective. While most kittens that are vaccinated will not contract the disease, there are exceptions. Here are several things that can happen to a vaccinated kitten that is subsequently exposed to a disease:

••➡ Most kittens will not contract the disease at all.

••➡ Some kittens will contract the virus or bacterium, shed the virus or bacterium, but never

---

••➡ If the pet jerks while receiving an injection, part of the vaccine might be injected into the air and not the pet. This means the pet must be revaccinated.

••➡ Most states only allow licensed veterinarians to obtain and give a rabies vaccination. Even if you give the other vaccinations yourself, you must still go to a veterinarian for a rabies vaccination. Many doctors charge a full office call just to give a rabies vaccinations.

••➡ By not using a veterinarian for all vaccinations, you deprive the pet of a yearly physical examination, heartworm test, and fecal analysis for parasites. *The* most important reason for the yearly visit is not the vaccinations but the examination. After all, how many pets do you know that die of rabies, parvo virus, or distemper infection? Very few. The most common causes of death are organ failure (especially heart, kidney, and liver), cancer, and systemic diseases secondary to periodontal infections. These are all things that can be discovered during the annual physical and in most cases successfully treated.

••➡ Finally, your pet will probably need to be boarded or hospitalized at some time. Unless you can show proof that a veterinarian has vaccinated the pet, both kennels and veterinary hospitals will require revaccination prior to boarding or hospitalization. This means an extra, unnecessary expense.

In the end, it really isn't worth it to attempt at-home vaccinations. There are other ways to save money on health care (see Chapter 13); don't put yourself and your pet at risk to save a few dollars.

appear ill. Yet, they can pass the virus or bacterium to other kittens.

••➡ Some kittens will get a mild form of the disease.

••➡ In very rare cases, the kitten will get the full-blown disease.

Vaccinations are important for all kittens and are an inexpensive way to prevent fatal diseases. Follow your doctor's recommendations for vaccinating your kitten.

Common Owner Concerns

Q: It seems like my kitten needs a lot of shots, and the doctor keeps giving her the same ones over and over. Are these additional vaccinations necessary?

A: Antibodies from the mother, called maternal antibodies, are present in any kitten whose mother was vaccinated prior to the pregnancy and who was able to nurse and receive colostrum. Maternal antibodies don't last forever. For some diseases, maternal antibodies disappear by eight weeks of age; for others, they may be present up to several months of age. While we know the average life of maternal antibodies, we don't know how long they last in any one individual kitten. We know if we vaccinate a kitten against parvo virus, for example, and maternal antibodies against parvo virus

are still present, that vaccine offers no protection (the maternal antibodies "interfere" with our vaccination). Since we don't know exactly when *your* kitten's maternal antibodies will disappear, we "overvaccinate" to be on the safe side. Too many vaccines will not hurt your kitten; undervaccinating it could be fatal. Therefore, veterinarians have developed vaccine protocols to maximize your kitten's ability to produce antibodies.

We also know that repeated vaccinations produce more antibodies than just one vaccination. Giving your kitten several vaccinations for the same disease allows it to produce maximum amount of antibodies, thus offering the most protection possible.

Q: My kitten seemed listless the day after she got her shots. Is this going to happen after every visit?

A: Some kittens seem to have more "vaccine reactions" than others. Usually, the reactions are mild and may include listlessness and a decreased appetite. Occasionally, a kitten may vomit or have diarrhea after the vaccination. Rarely, repeated vomiting, diarrhea, difficulty breathing, or hives may be seen. If any of these more severe signs occur, your kitten should receive immediate treatment for this allergic reaction.

A kitten that has a reaction after a vaccination will not necessarily have one every time. As the kitten grows, the incidences of vaccine reactions usually decrease or disappear.

Q: After the vaccination, my kitten had a lump on her hip for about three weeks. What caused this?

A: Vaccines are foreign proteins, or antigens. Since the body recognizes vaccines as antigens, a local inflammatory response occurs. The lump you saw was a result of this local inflammation and is called a sterile abscess. As the inflammation subsides and the foreign protein is absorbed and neutralized, the lump should disappear as the body heals itself. These abscesses usually require no treatment and are not painful to your kitten. If there is any doubt as to whether the lump is from the vaccine, the doctor can aspirate the lump and examine it microscopically to determine the cause.

Chapter 4
The First Doctor Visit

· ·

Ideally, you should have your new kitten examined the day of purchase. If your doctor's office is not open the day you purchase your kitten, at least try to schedule the first visit within 24 to 48 hours. It's critical to make sure your kitten is healthy, especially if the party who sold you the kitten gives you a health warranty good for several days following the purchase.

During the first visit, your kitten will probably need some vaccinations. Which vaccinations your kitten will need depends upon whether or not he has had any previous vaccinations and how old he is when you purchase him. Specific vaccinations are discussed in chapters 3 and 12.

The doctor will do several things on the first visit; depending upon whether any illnesses are detected during the visit and how many questions you have, the first visit will take anywhere from 30 to 60 minutes. During the first visit, the vet will:

●●➡ Perform a complete physical examination.

●●➡ Do a microscopic analysis of the feces ("stool test") for internal parasites.

●●➡ Discuss feeding, training, behavior, spaying or neutering, heartworm disease, and what will occur during subsequent visits.

●●➡ Answer any questions you may ask.

The Physical Exam

An important part of the visit is the physical examination. This exam is done to determine if your kitten is healthy enough to receive vaccinations, as well as determine if any illnesses or congenital abnormalities exist. If problems are found during the exam, you may desire to return the kitten to the breeder or pet store for a replacement or payment for medical services as allowed by your contract or warranty.

During the exam, the doctor will:

•••➡ Examine the ears, checking for any unusual odors or exudate (waxy buildup) that might indicate an infection with ear mites, bacteria, and/or yeasts (Chapter 10).

•••➡ Examine the eyes. They should be clear; the sclera (white part of the eyes) should be white, not red, and have a few small blood vessels present. There should be no large amounts of

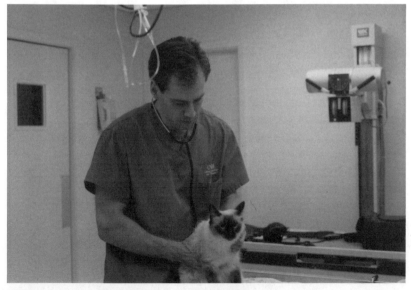

The doctor listens to the heart and lungs for signs of a heart murmur or respiratory infection during the annual physical examination.

discharge; any drainage that is seen should be clear (some breeds of kittens such as Persians and Himalyans normally have a small amount of drainage from the eyes).

••➡ Look in the mouth. The doctor wants to be sure the deciduous teeth (baby teeth) are growing in normally, and that the upper and lower teeth touch when the mouth is closed. Abnormalities of the teeth or jaws may require orthodontic correction. The hard palate is examined to make sure that a cleft palate is not present. The odor of the mouth is noted; foul odors may indicate an oral infection.

••➡ Check the skin and hair coat. There should be no external parasites such as fleas or ticks on

---

DOES YOUR PET REALLY HAVE A FEVER? . . . .

From time to time you may need to take your kitten's temperature. It's not a difficult procedure, although most owners find it at least a little unpleasant (and kittens find it a bit uncomfortable).

To take your kitten's temperature, purchase a thermometer (preferably one that goes to 106 degrees) and some lubricant (such as K-Y Jelly or even Vasoline). Have someone hold the kitten's head and body, carefully restraining him. Insert the lubricated thermometer about one inch into the kitten's rectum and hold it in place for approximately two minutes. (Have your veterinarian demonstrate this for you before you attempt it for the first time.) When the time is up, remove the thermometer and record the temperature. Be sure to clean the thermometer well and label it for the kitten's use only!

Normal temperature for a kitten is 101.5 (with a range of 100.5-102.5). If the temperature is 103.5 or higher, call your veterinarian. If it is 104 or higher, plan on visiting the doctor.

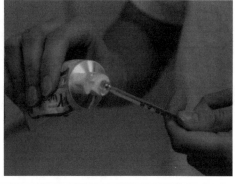

the kitten. No bald spots should be present. The hair should be smooth and shiny, and not rough and unkempt. The skin should be free of lumps, bumps, pimples, and any other skin lesions that might indicate an infection, such as mange or ringworm (Chapter 10).

••➡ Palpate (feel) the abdomen. No pain should be noted during the palpation, nor should any organs feel enlarged. The umbili-cal (belly-button) area is examined for the presence of a hernia (Chapter 11) that may need surgical correction.

••➡ Listen to the heart and lungs. Occasionally a heart murmur is present, or the heart can't be heard normally on one side of the chest. A murmur is caused by turbulent blood flow in the heart or blood vessels leading from the heart. Heart murmurs in

WORMS . . . .

Worms are often blamed for many kitten illnesses. While worms can be a problem, other conditions can cause similar diseases.

Worms, more correctly called internal parasites, are often found in the microscopic examination of your kitten's feces. Rarely, worms can actually be seen in the kitten's stool. The most common type of worms that owners actually see in the feces are either roundworms, which look like spaghetti and are only seen in severe infections, or tapeworms, which are flat, resemble grains of rice, and are caused by fleas.

Sometimes, kittens with worms, usually tapeworms, will scoot their rumps on the floor, although scooting is more often seen with anal sac problems (which is rare in kittens compared to puppies).

Regular microscopic examinations of your kitten's feces will help ensure that your kitten stays worm-free. Because so many things can cause diseases in kittens other than internal parasites, owners should refrain from using over-the-counter deworming medications which are often ineffective anyway. If your kitten requires it, regular use of monthly heartworm preventative medication can help control internal parasites.

KEEPING YOUR PET CLEAN . . . .

New kitten owners often ask if they should bathe their kittens. Usually the kitten only needs to be bathed when he gets dirty or smelly (except for those breeds that require regular grooming). Most veterinarians generally suggest no more than weekly bathing unless the kitten has a skin problem requiring more frequent bathing.

A popular shampoo is HyLyt shampoo, available from your veterinarian. This shampoo is mild, hypoallergenic, soap-free, and contains moisturizers. All of this means that regular bathing won't dry out your kitten's delicate skin like harsher shampoos can. And remember not to use people shampoo unless it's an emergency and your veterinarian okays it. Human products are formulated for human skin, which is structurally different from kitten skin.

Start bathing your kitten when he is young (6-8 weeks) so he will become used to the bathing procedure. Try to make it as pleasant an experience as possible. A tub or a sink works fine: massage water into the coat, use the shampoo, and thoroughly rinse him. If shampoo gets in the kitten's eyes, thoroughly flush them out with water. Drying with a towel or blow dryer is fine. Kittens will not chill and get sick after bathing, so don't be concerned about that.

Most kittens seem to mind the *sound* of the rushing water more than the water itself. If you will fill up the tub or sink first, and then use a cup to pour water on your kitten, this may be more comfortable for him than letting the water run while he's in the tub or sink.

kittens can be innocent (also called physiologic) murmurs or pathologic murmurs. Innocent murmurs (Chapter 11) are soft murmurs that normally disappear by six months of age and will not cause the kitten any problem. Pathologic murmurs can be caused by fever, anemia, or problems with the heart valves or blood vessels leading from the heart.

●●➡ Examine the genital system. While most male kittens will have both of their testes in the scrotum by the first visit, some do not. These will often descend by the last visit; if they do not, surgery is needed to neuter the pet and correct the cryptorchid condition (Chapter 11).

Microscopic Fecal Examination

A fresh (less than 24 hours old) sample of your kitten's feces will be examined microscopically for the presence of intestinal parasites (worms). You should plan on bringing a fecal sample to the veterinarian; although he can often obtain one from your kitten, the procedure is a bit uncomfortable (similar to taking its temperature). The feces should be fresh; it's advised to collect it the day before your actual appointment (if you wait until the day of the appointment, the kitten may not eliminate and then you won't have a sample! If you already have a sample and the kitten provides you with a fresh one right before your visit, you can always dispose of the older sample and bring the fresh one). Only a *small* sample is needed, roughly one-half teaspoonful. Some owners get a bit overzealous and bring in quite a lot of feces. This is one case where more is definitely *not* better!

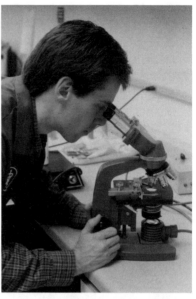

Fecal material is microscopically examined for worms and other parasites.

The doctor will mix the feces with a sodium nitrate solution that will cause any parasite eggs present to float to the top of the vial, where they are trapped on a glass slide. The slide is then examined microscopically for the eggs.

Alternatively, if a very small sample of feces is available, the doctor may perform a direct smear of the feces on a microscope slide mixed with a drop of water. This test is not as accurate as the flotation but can often detect any eggs that are present. If your kitten has had diarrhea, the doctor may do a floatation

OTC MEDICATIONS............................

In an attempt to save money on veterinary visits, many owners play doctor at home and give their kittens human medications. While many human drugs are used in kittens, this practice should only be done under veterinary supervision. Many human products are not safe for use in pets. Also, pets require different doses than people. Commonly used over-the-counter medications include:

••➡ Aspirin. Aspirin can be used in cats but due to the long "half-life" and increased toxicity, a very low dose must be used. Also, aspirin can only be given once every 72 hours to avoid toxicity.

••➡ Non-steroidals. Non-steroidal medications, such as ibuprofen, Advil, or Naprosyn are commonly taken by people for headaches, menstrual cramps, arthritis, and any type of musculoskeletal pain. These drugs are extremely dangerous in cats; many cats have been poisoned and killed by well-intentioned owners who treated their pets with their own medicines. These drugs should not be used in cats; veterinarians rarely prescribe them, and only if other drugs are ineffective and the pet is closely monitored.

••➡ Tylenol. Another drug which kills cats, Tylenol is often used by owners who suspect that their pet has a fever. Fevers are the body's way of protecting itself and should only be controlled if excessively high with medication prescribed by your doctor.

••➡ Antidiarrheals. Pepto Bismol and Kaopectate can be used safely in most kittens if directed by your veterinarian. However, they are generally ineffective for most causes of diarrhea and can be messy to administer. Until your veterinarian has determined the cause of the diarrhea, it's best not to treat the kitten with home remedies.

••➡ Cough medications. While some doctors okay using human cough syrups at home, coughing in kittens is usually associated with respiratory infections or internal parasites; cough medicines are likely to be ineffective in these instances.

Always check with your veterinarian before treating your pet at home. While many over-the-counter medications can be used safely, your doctor needs to be aware of any signs of illness in your kitten.

and a smear to increase the chances of finding the eggs.

Owners are often surprised that a doctor may want to run more than one fecal sample. Many doctors check the feces at each kitten visit, some check it just once, and some check a sample on the first and last kitten visit. Worms are not continuously laying eggs; it may be that your kitten has worms but they were not laying eggs the particular day that the feces were checked. Failure to check the feces again could mean that your kitten has worms but they were missed due to the one negative sample.

Discussion of Kitten Information

Unless you have other cats, you probably don't know much about your new kitten. While books, breeders, pet store employees, and well-intentioned friends may feel they know it all, your veterinarian has received years of training in school and post doctoral continuing education in his field. He is uniquely qualified to instruct you on the proper care of your new kitten. Take the advice from others with a grain of salt; these well-intentioned friends might think they know it all, but they have not received formal training in veterinary

STEROIDS . . . .

A class of drugs commonly used by veterinarians is the corticosteroids. These drugs are used for many conditions, including reducing inflammation, relieving the pain of arthritis, treating animals in shock, treating cancers and autoimmune diseases, and relieving the itchiness associated with many types of allergic diseases. These are not the same class of steroids that is discussed in the media, namely the anabolic steroids taken by athletes for improved performance.

While corticosteroids are truly wonder drugs that can relieve many problems in cats, they have disadvantages. Common short-term side effects include increased appetite, increased thirst, and increased urination (although these side effects are less common in cats than in dogs). Rarely, some cats will act "spaced out,"

medicine. Follow your doctor's advice when it comes to caring for your new family member!

Several areas of concern should be discussed during the visit. These include selecting litter, biting, general kitten behavior problems, spaying or neutering versus breeding, a lifeplan for your kitten, an explanation of what vaccinations need to be given and when, heartworm disease and prevention, bathing, brushing the kitten's teeth, grooming needs, including home care of nails and coat, feeding, vitamins, parasite control (if needed), and any other concerns that may affect your kitten.

Ask Questions

You are paying for the doctor's time, so make the most of your visit. Bring a list of questions for the doctor. No question is stupid! Even though the doctor may have heard the question before, *you* have never asked it before, and you deserve an answer. If your doctor rushes you or refuses to answer questions, it's time to look for another doctor!

hyperexcitable, or even lethargic or drunk. These side effects wear off shortly after the medication is stopped.

Long-term side effects from chronic use include osteoporosis, liver disease, diabetes, decreased wound healing, increased susceptibility to infections, Cushing's disease (a condition of too much steroid in the body) and Addison's disease (a shock-like condition that occurs if steroids, which have been used chronically, are suddenly stopped).

Long-term side effects can be prevented by treating the pet with other medications if they are available, such as antihistamines in allergic conditions. In cases where corticosteroids need to be used for a long period of time (cancers, autoimmune diseases like lupus), the pet is carefully monitored and the lowest effective dose possible is used. If your veterinarian prescribes "steroids" for your pet, be sure to discuss the pros and cons and side effects of the medication.

APPROVED MEDICATIONS. . . . .

It may surprise pet owners to know that many medications used by veterinarians are not "approved" for use in pets. Does this mean that doctors are using drugs that might harm your pet? Is your pet in danger from these "unapproved" medications?

For a drug to get FDA approval, the drug company that manufactures the drug often spends millions of dollars putting the drug through numerous tests for safety and efficacy. This would be cost-prohibitive for most drug companies. Instead, many veterinary colleges and research institutions attempt to discern accurate dosages for pets based upon how the drug is used in people. Through research at these institutions, veterinarians determine if the drug works in pets, if it is safe, and at what dosage the drug can be used.

Many of the drugs we use in pets have not gone through the expensive procedures required by the FDA. As an example, the antihistamine Benadryl, often used in allergic cats, does not have an FDA label approval for cats. The Benadryl your doctor prescribes for your allergic dog is the same drug you would take for allergies (at a different dosage though). There will probably never be a "kitty" Benadryl; the makers of Benadryl are not going to spend a lot of money getting label approval for cats when they know the drug works in cats and is used by many veterinarians regularly.

If doctors did not use "unapproved" drugs in their practices, many pets would suffer and die needlessly. As long as the doctor understands the pharmacology of the drug, it is safe for him to use in pets.

Your pet will not serve as a guinea pig for an experimental therapy unless your doctor discusses this with you and gets your approval first. While many people drugs are used regularly by veterinarians for pets, you should never administer medications you are taking for your pet without discussing this with your doctor first.

GIVING YOUR KITTEN MEDICINE . . . .

Giving your kitten a tablet.

Liquid medicines are easily administered with a syringe.

Common Owner Concerns

Q: The breeder has already given my kitten her first set of shots, yet the doctor wants to revaccinate her. Is there a need for this extra expense?

A: Some doctors feel the need to revaccinate kittens that have already had some vaccinations. It may be that your doctor doesn't trust the particular breeder who sold you your kit-

ten. Maybe he feels that breeder used the incorrect vaccine, or that it was given at too early an age. If you trust your doctor, rest assured that he isn't revaccinating your new kitten just to make a few extra dollars. If you are uncomfortable and don't trust him, you may want to consider looking for another veterinarian for your pet. Remember, though, that the doctor does know more about health care than any breeder, so I would tend to believe him over a breeder or other pet supplier.

Q: Is it really necessary that our kitten have an examination on every visit? She seems healthy and the examinations are just another expense. This kitten is costing us a lot of money!

A: You are beginning to realize just how expensive owning a kitten actually can be for its owner. Hopefully, all potential kitten owners will do their homework *before* purchasing their pet and make sure they can afford the care required by this new family member.

A complete physical examination is critical on each and every visit. Your kitten is rapidly growing and changing. Problems not present on the previous examinations may become apparent on future visits. Realize that the most important part of every veterinary visit is the examination and not the vaccinations. Take advantage of each visit to discuss any questions or concerns you have about your kitten's health or behavior.

TOYS

Kittens love toys, and it seems most owners love buying toys for their kittens. Try to offer a variety of play things for your pet, and keep the following points in mind:

••➡ Make sure the size of the item fits the size of the pet; don't offer a kitten anything small enough to be easily swallowed or an item that might be chewed into smaller pieces that can be swallowed.

••➡ Avoid stuffed toys that are easily destroyed. Many kittens can develop intestinal obstructions from the stuffing. Also avoid toys with pieces that can easily come off (such as eyes on a doll) and be swallowed.

••➡ Kittens are teething for the first six months of their lives and *need* to chew; it's better they chew on toys than on you or the furniture!

••➡ Use care with string. While kittens love to chase and play with string, when it is swallowed, the string can cut the intestines. This can be rapidly fatal to your kitten and requires surgery to correct.

Chapter 5
Feeding Your Kitten

. . . .

Three of the most common questions new kitten owners ask are "What do I feed my kitten," "How often do I feed him," and "How much do I feed him?" The simple and correct answers are, respectively, "Premium kitten food," "Feed as often as he gets hungry," and "Feed him as much as he needs to eat"! Unfortunately, these answers don't offer a lot of help to new owners. In order to answer these questions, it's first necessary to understand something about pet food. While you don't need a Ph.D. in nutrition to properly feed your kitten, it does make sense to have a basic understanding of nutrition to ensure that your kitten will get everything it needs.

Nutrients

Your kitten needs many nutrients to not only sustain life but to encourage growth, promote a healthy coat, and allow proper function of its organs and immune system. An improperly nourished kitten is unhealthy and is prone to illness. Preventing illness with proper nutrition is an important part of a pet owner's responsibility.

Water While most people forget about water as a nutrient, it is without a doubt the most important one. An animal can survive after losing most of its fat or protein, but a 15 percent loss of body water results in death! Your kitten's body, just like your body, is made up mostly of water. While food can supply a little or a lot of the kitten's daily water needs, your pet should always have a fresh bowl of clean water. An exception might be made when housebreaking your new kitten—you may decide to remove water from its cage at night. That's fine, as long as water was available throughout the day and will be offered in the morning.

Dry food is 6 to 10 percent water, soft-moist is 23 to 40 percent water, and canned food is 68 to 78 percent water. As a rule, the amount of water consumed by mature cats is about 2.5 times the amount of dry matter consumed in food.

Water should be increased in times of illness, when fever is present, when the temperature increases, if your kitten pants excessively, or if certain medications (such as corticosteroids) are given which result in an increased urinary output.

Energy For simplicity's sake, energy is provided in food by fats, carbohydrates, and proteins. The energy content of food is defined in kilocalories, which is 1,000 calories (in nutrition language, the word calorie usually means kilocalorie). If the food is a premium food and correctly

balanced, as a rule feeding the amount needed to meet the kitten's energy requirement provides the proper amount of all its needed nutrients. The amount to feed can be calculated by dividing the animal's energy requirement by the energy density of the food. In practice, most owners don't wish to do this. Pet food companies have already done this and offer a suggested amount to feed on the food package; the amount varies with the pet's weight.

Carbohydrates Carbohydrates are composed of sugars, starches, and fiber. Carbohydrates are excellent sources of energy in kitten foods. Excess carbohydrates in the diet that are not needed by the kitten are stored as body fat.

Fiber is used to add bulk to the diet to prevent both diarrhea and constipation. Fiber also helps the animal feel full so it doesn't become obese. Cheaper pet foods often have too much fiber; kittens become full before consuming the needed nutrients and can exhibit nutritional deficiencies.

Protein Protein is composed of amino acids, which are the "building blocks" of the body.

Proteins are used as enzymes, hormones, and in making muscle and other structural tissues. While people often mistakenly are concerned about the protein content of food, in reality it's the amino acids that are important. The protein sources used in formulating the diet must contain the proper amounts of the essential amino acids needed by the pet, or it will suffer from an amino acid deficiency despite an adequate protein intake.

Unlike dogs, cats are true carnivores and require a diet high in protein, much higher than is required for dogs. Depending upon the age and metabolic activity of the pet, kittens and cats require about 25-35 percent protein. Cats also require the amino acid taurine. This amino acid is necessary to prevent retinal degeneration, which can lead to blindness, and has also been shown to prevent the dilated form of cardiomyopathy, a fatal heart condition. Finally, cats also require more niacin in their diets as well as preformed vitamin A. These are important reasons why kittens and cats should only eat diets designed specifically for felines; feeding cats dog food can be fatal.

Fat Fats are used for energy as well as being needed for the absorption of vitamins A, D, E, and K. Fats also are used in the body's productions of hormones. Fats also make diets more palatable. Excess concentrations of fats can lead to obesity, hepatic lipidosis (fatty liver disease), and pancreatitis.

Fat deficiency, or rather fatty acid deficiency, is rare in pets. Certain fatty acids can be supplemented by your doctor to help with certain skin problems, specifically atopic dermatitis, a form of allergic dermatitis.

Minerals Minerals include such things as calcium, phosphorus, iron, and zinc, among others. As a rule, minerals function as co-enzymes which help control numerous biochemical reactions in the body. Minerals also are constituents of bone and muscle. Mineral deficiencies rarely occur in pets, with the exception of zinc deficiency (see below). Mineral excess can occur by overzealous administration of minerals by owners, specifically calcium and phosphorus. Many owners give their growing kittens calcium pills, thinking it will help with skeletal growth. Too much calcium can actually cause problems. Mineral supplementation is not recommended unless directed by your veterinarian.

Zinc deficiency can result from excess dietary calcium (seen when owners supplement kitten food with calcium pills) or in cheap, generic pet foods. Many cheap pet foods are deficient in zinc; kittens that eat this diet usually show signs of zinc deficiency, which include crusty, scaly skin. In people, a similar condition is called acrodermatitis enteropathica. The disease in kittens often occurs with cheap, generic foods that contain excess calcium, phytic acid (common in plant proteins which make up a large part of generic diets), copper, and cadmium. These substances bind the zinc in the diet, reducing its absorption by the intestines. The disease may only be seen in kittens eating certain lots of generic foods, as generic foods vary in their nutritional content from lot to lot (another reason generic foods are very inexpensive and inadequate nutritionally for your kitten). Treatment involves zinc supplementation and switching to a premium diet.

Vitamins Like minerals, vitamins function as enzymes or co-enzymes. Pure vitamin deficiencies or toxicities are rarely encountered in kittens, as pet food manufacturers "overcompensate" and make sure the food contains more than enough of these compounds. There are a few rare exceptions: Vitamin A toxicity can result during the course of treating a certain type of skin disease, vitamin A deficiency seborrhea. This disease is rare and usually would occur in an older cat. Owners treating this condition under a doctor's guidance are warned about the signs of vitamin A toxicity so treatment can be altered at the first signs of problems.

Vitamin K deficiency can rarely occur as a result of chronic diarrhea, acute poisoning by warfarin-type rat poisons, if poor-quality diets are fed which contain an insufficient amount of fat, and as a result of certain antibiotic therapy.

Thiamine deficiency can result in pets fed exclusively fish diets

Large amounts of ingested raw egg whites can result in a biotin deficiency; however, this is also rare.

Which Brand of Food?

Now that you have a basic understanding of nutrition, the next step is to understand the differences in pet foods. Some seem to cost a lot, whereas others are extremely inexpensive. With so many choices, how do you know what food is right for your kitten? Can reading the labels help, or are they another source of confusion?

While breeders, groomers, and clerks at the pet stores all have their own opinions about the "best" brand of food, realize that once again your doctor has been trained in nutrition. He is the best source to turn to for nutritional advice.

However, doctors can also be biased. Due to intense competition from the large number of veterinarians, doctors feel pressure to sell pet food in their offices as well. You could easily assume that your doctor is biased toward the brand he sells. There may be some truth to that; your doctor has a variety of brands he could choose to sell. Most doctors do their homework and select one to several brands they feel are the best.

In deciding what food is best for your kitten, realize that all kittens are different. What is best for your kitten may not be best for your neighbor's kitten. The neighbor's pet may not find your kitten's food palatable; maybe your kitten's food even makes the neighbor's pet sick. Obviously, consulting with a doctor to find the right choice of food makes sense.

Grocery Store, Pet Store, Discount Store, or Doctor's Office? There are several classifications of foods available for your kitten. Generic or private-label foods are the least expensive but also least healthy for your pet. Owners should avoid this type of food, as health problems such as zinc or fatty acid deficiency may result.

Grocery stores carry popular brands of food, such as those made by Gaines, Purina, and Kennel Ration, among others. Most of these foods have been around for years, have undergone extensive research and feeding trials, and are acceptable choices of foods for your kitten.

Premium foods are available at many pet stores and veterinary hospitals. They have the highest-quality ingredients available in pet foods; therefore, they tend to be the most expensive.

Obviously, there are many sources competing for your pet

food dollar. Choosing a pet food is important and should not be done hastily. It would even be wise to discuss the choice with your veterinarian *before* you purchase your kitten. Having to buy food on the spur of the moment after purchasing the kitten is not a good idea.

The price of pet foods is determined by many things. These include marketing and advertising, feeding trials, and quality of ingredients. The *cost* of pet foods, which is different from the *price* of the foods, is exactly how much it costs to feed the pet at each meal. The cost of the food is really more

YOU CAN'T JUDGE A LABEL BY WHAT IT SAYS . . . .

Many clients say that they feed a particular brand of pet food based on the advice of a breeder, groomer, or pet store clerk. While these sources are well intentioned and may have a favorite brand, they are not doctors. Veterinarians receive formal training in nutrition and diseases that can result from improper nutrition. Take your veterinarian's advice on the proper food for your pet. Kittens require one type of food, adult animals another, and geriatric pets still another.

Be careful what the label says too. Many clients tell me that the label on their brand of food claims it is nutritionally complete and therefore are convinced it must be a good food. Here are a few tips on reading the pet food labels.

1. *Guaranteed Analysis.* This states the minimum levels of nutrients in the food. A food with a minimum level of 5 percent protein means that the food has at least 5 percent protein; it may have a lot more, possibly even too much! Also, there is no guarantee that this protein is a good-quality protein. Chicken feathers have at least 5 percent protein, but I promise you that your pet won't get any nutrients from this protein source!

2. *Digestibility.* Poultry meal is a common protein source, but the digestibility of protein meals varies from poor to excellent.

important than the price. For example, a generic brand of food has a lower price than a premium brand, but actually costs more. Why? Let's suppose that due to the high bulk content of the generic food, a 10-pound bag lasts only two weeks for your pet because he has to eat so much of it to get his required daily energy. Let's suppose that same 10-pound bag of premium food lasts eight weeks; because of the high-quality ingredients, the pet doesn't need to eat as much. The price of the premium food may be more for each bag, but because it lasts longer the cost is lower. With the premium food, there will probably be less

Reputable manufacturers use higher-quality ingredients; the quality of the ingredient is reflected in the cost of the food. Stay away from poorly digestible, cheaper generic brands.

3. *Nutritional Adequacy.* Many products state that the food has been "formulated to meet the nutrition levels established by the AAFCO." Unfortunately, this just guarantees the food meets a mathematical minimum number. Your pet may not be able to digest or absorb anything in it, because the food never had to go through feeding trials to assess palatability, digestibility, and nutritional merit.

"Animal feeding tests using AAFCO procedures that substantiate that this food provides complete and balanced nutrition" means the food has been fed to many pets for extended periods of time and that no nutritional problems were detected. The better, more expensive brands use this designation after conducting costly feeding trials.

4. *Cost.* There's nothing wrong with trying to save a buck *if* you're not putting your pet's health at risk. A recent survey of pet foods showed that a premium brand costs no more than the average cost of the nine most popular grocery store brands.

Unfortunately, you can't rely on the label to differentiate between pet foods. Your veterinarian has been trained in nutrition. Follow his advice when determining the proper food for your pets. Usually, the cost of the diets at his office are very competitive with pet stores and in some cases even cheaper.

feces produced each day (a desirable quality for pet owners). Feeding premium food may result in fewer doctor bills since the food is a better diet for the pet. While the cost of the ingredients in premium diets is higher than in generic diets, the health benefits and the smaller amount of food needed at each feeding compensate for the higher-priced ingredients.

There is some concern about whether these premium foods actually result in better health than the popular grocery store brands. There is no current research to show the extra benefit when compared to popular store brands that have undergone similar testing (feeding trials). However, due to intense competition the price difference between premium brands and popular brands is fairly small.

In helping you and your doctor decide whether a premium brand or popular brand should be offered, consider that the main difference is quality of ingredients. A typical premium brand might have whole dressed chicken as a main ingredient, whereas the popular brand might contain chicken parts or by-products. While chicken by-products are not bad, the nutritional value

is not quite as good as whole chicken.

These are just some of the factors to consider when deciding if a premium food is best for your kitten or if you would prefer a popular store brand. There are other factors to consider when selecting a food, however.

Palatability No matter how good the nutrients are in a particular kitten food, he must eat it! While that may sound obvious, not every kitten likes every food. Palatability is a measure of how tasty a particular food is. Several factors influence the palatability of a food:

••➡ Food temperature—Food warmed to body temperature is more palatable than food at room temperature; warming the food is often advised for kittens that don't seem interested in a food or when the kitten is ill. Warming only works for canned food; warm water can be added to dry food for a similar effect.

••➡ Odor—Cats have an excellent sense of smell so the food must smell good for the pet to eat it. Pets with blocked nasal passages (from illness) may not be able to smell the food and may not eat it. Warming increases odor.

• •➡ Texture—Some pets prefer a certain feel or shape of food; because of its texture, canned food is always preferred over dry food.

• •➡ Nutrient content—Foods with a higher fat content are preferred over foods that are high in fiber, so-called diet foods.

• •➡ Habit—Most pets prefer the diet to which they are accustomed; new foods should be introduced slowly.

Acceptability Just because a food is palatable doesn't mean your kitten will accept it. In order for food to be accepted, the kitten must obviously be hungry and have a need for the food. Additionally, the kitten must not show an aversion to the food. If the food previously made the kitten sick, he may not want to eat it.

Optimum Nutrient Content Foods available for sale must list on the bag that the food met guidelines established by the AAFCO (Association of American Feed Control Officials). The AAFCO statement will either say that the diet has been "formulated to meet the nutrition levels established by the AAFCO" or "animal feeding tests using AAFCO procedures substantiate that this food provides complete and balanced nutrition."

CHANGING FOODS . . . .

You rarely have to offer your kitten a different brand of food, but there's nothing wrong with doing so if you want to offer the kitten variety. However, there is a secret to switching brands of food. Switching to a new brand overnight may cause vomiting or diarrhea in a few cats; some pets are finicky and may not eat a new diet that is suddenly introduced.

The best way to offer your pet a new diet is by gradually introducing it. When you have about a week's worth of the old diet remaining, purchase the new food. Add about 10 percent of the new diet each day, gradually adding more until you run out of the old food and the pet is eating only the new diet. This trick usually prevents upset tummies and eases the transition to the new food.

LAMB AND RICE...
NOT ALWAYS THE BEST CHOICE ....

Recently, many pet owners have jumped on the "lamb and rice" bandwagon. Pet food manufacturers, in their attempts to sell yet another type of food, have pushed lamb and rice diets as the newest, best things for pets. A big selling point is that these diets are "hypoallergenic"; by feeding them, your pet should never have food allergies.

While there is nothing inherently wrong with lamb and rice diets, there are some things to consider before spending extra money on this special diet:

••➡ Food allergies are extremely rare in pets; less than 10 percent of kittens and cats will ever develop a food allergy.

Unfortunately, food that just meets nutrition levels may not be adequate for your kitten. This designation just guarantees the food meets a mathematical minimum. Your pet may not be able to digest or absorb anything in it, because the food never had to go through feeding trials to assess palatability and digestibility or show if the animals in the trials grew or suffered malnutrition.

Diets that have gone through extensive feeding trials often cost more than generic foods but are preferred. Food that has been tested through feeding trials has been fed to many pets for extended periods of time with no nutritional problem detected.

Supplementation Premium diets are complete and balanced and do not need to be supplemented with "people food." While some pets suffer no ill effects from eating small amounts of certain people foods, other pets don't do as well. Many pets can develop diarrhea or vomit after eating food other than their own. Some pets can develop pancreatitis, an often fatal disease than can be brought on by eating foods high in fat content. Also, some human foods can be toxic, such as chocolate, or hard for the pet to digest, such as milk. Unless your doctor advises otherwise, avoid giving your kitten people food and offer it only premium-quality kitten food.

••➡ There is nothing inherently hypoallergenic about lamb or rice. Food allergies are more likely to be caused by a protein source that the pet has been eating for some time, often several years. Assuming your kitten is never exposed to lamb, he'll never develop an allergy to lamb. However, if you start feeding him a lamb-based diet, he can certainly become allergic to lamb later in life.

••➡ Pets diagnosed with food allergies need a hypoallergenic diet. If your pet is used to eating lamb, it will be difficult and expensive to find a suitable diet. Other diet choices for pets with food allergies include fish, turkey, shrimp, lobster, or venison.

••➡ Many lamb and rice diets also contain egg, wheat, soy, beef, and chicken. Your kitten could develop allergies to any or all of these substances despite eating a "lamb and rice" diet.

Since your kitten doesn't derive any extra nutritional benefit from lamb, save your money and feed him a diet recommended by your doctor. If he is ever diagnosed with a food allergy, then your veterinarian may recommend a lamb-based diet as a treatment.

Prozyme   Prozyme is an enzyme supplement that contains cellulase, among other enzymes. Cellulase breaks down cellulose, a constituent of plant cell walls. Since plant material can be found as a component in all pet foods, it is theorized that prozyme might make some nutrients available to the kitten by breaking down these cell walls. Many doctors recommend Prozyme as a way to increase the digestion and absorption of nutrients in the pet's food. Keep in mind that no nutritional supplement will improve a poor-quality diet. As with any nutritional supplement, Prozyme should not be given to your pet without discussing it with your veterinarian.

Additives   Some pet owners who fear additives look for additive-free food. Recent research, however, confirms what doctors have said all along: additives rarely cause any problem—they account for 5 percent or less of food-sensitivity problems in pets. The recent use of additive-free foods has resulted in an increase of food poisoning in people and pets, however.

How Often To Feed

Most people leave food down all day for their kittens and cats. Since kittens and cats usually nibble many small meals during the day, this free-choice method of feeding simulates their normal feeding behavior. Owners who like to feed dry and canned food will usually leave dry food available 24 hours a day and offer a spoon or two of canned food in the morning and in the evening. Unless your cat develops obesity or has a medical condition, free-choice feeding is used more often with cats than meal feeding.

Obesity

While obesity is extremely rare in kittens less than one year old, it is something that can occur or be prevented as a result of feeding habits and behavioral patterns established during kittenhood.

Surprisingly, obesity is the most common nutritional disease in pets, as in people. It is estimated that up to 45 percent of cats are affected. It seems to occur in neutered cats more than in intact cats, especially in spayed females. Owners who are overweight are also more likely to have overweight pets. Older, single people, who overfeed their pets as an act of kindness or of spoiling them (killing their pets with kindness), also seem to have more of a problem with obese pets than the general population.

Obesity is usually defined as a body weight of 15 percent above the ideal body weight. While that doesn't seem like a lot, consider that a cat whose ideal body weight should be 10 pounds would be obese if he weighed just 11.5 pounds! Owners who feel that their cats weigh just a little too much don't realize that for some cats, weighing a little too much could equate with being dangerously obese.

You can easily feel the ribs of a normal cat who has just a small amount of body fat. Difficulty in feeling the ribs indicates obesity. If you are unable to feel your pet's ribs, it is dangerously obese.

Diets high in fat or sugar are more likely to result in obesity. Obesity results when the excess energy in the diet is stored by an increase in either the number or size of the fat cells. Since the number of fat cells can increase primarily during pregnancy through six months of life, overfeeding kittens increases their fat cell numbers, which makes them prone to obesity later in life. It is recommended to avoid overfeeding; a slightly thin kitten is preferable to an overweight kitten. Excess energy intake must be prevented during this six-month growth phase.

In obese pets, the overall energy expenditure is decreased; some obese pets maintain obesity on a diet which contains fewer calories than the diet of their normal weight counterparts. In essence, their body weight setpoints are lowered as a result of obesity. This is the reason that obese pets have a lot of trouble losing weight even on store-bought "lite" diets and must be placed on a medically supervised diet that is severely restricted in calories.

Obesity can also be caused by certain hormonal conditions in cats. Some of the hormonal problems that should be investigated as a cause of obesity include low thyroid levels (hypothyroidism, which is very rare in cats), high cortisol levels (seen in a disease called hyperadrenocorticism, which usually results from a tumor or enlargement of the adrenal glands), pancreatic tumors, or low sex hormones after neutering or spaying. It should be pointed out that neutering and spaying per se do *not* result in weight gain. Rather, the

removal of the sex hormones may be associated with a decreased energy expenditure. Failing to decrease food intake after neutering or spaying may result in obesity.

Complications of obesity can include diabetes, hypertension (a disease that is only now being recognized frequently in cats), liver disease, abnormal drug metabolism (which can result in toxic levels of normally "safe" medications as well as prolonged recovery from anesthesia), cardiovascular disease, decreased respiratory capacity (which can increase the risk of anesthesia and strenuous exercise), bone and joint problems (arthritis), cancer, reduced resistance to disease, and dermatitis.

Controlling obesity and preventing its recurrence involve feeding a diet severely restricted in energy under the supervision of your veterinarian. Moderately increase exercise (not always easy in cats which are normally sedentary) and alter your owner/pet behavior (eliminate begging and the need for treats, don't feed your pet at the table, etc.) are important. Starvation, feeding your pet "a little less," is not recommended; this practice is dangerous and usually results in a decreased ratio of muscle tissue to fat. Using store-bought "lite" diets usually fails to reduce the weight but may, in a few selected instances, help maintain the reduced weight once the ideal weight has been reached. Exercise without calorie restriction is not effective in yielding significant weight loss.

Common Owner Concerns

Q: Does my kitten really need vitamins?

A: Assuming your kitten is eating a high-quality diet, which contains ample vitamins and minerals, he does not need additional vitamins. As with people, however, administering one or two kitten vitamin tablets each day will not harm the pet (as long as your doctor okays it). While he does not *need* the vitamins, kittens also do not *need* treats, yet most owners give their kittens all sorts of treats. Since one or two kitten vitamins a day won't hurt the kitten, offering him this low-fat, low-salt alternative to store-bought treats will ensure that he receives all the vitamins and minerals he needs (especially if his food intake is down a bit because of hot weather or a minor illness), and is an excellent way to reinforce the kitten-owner bond that is so critical to establish between owners and pets. It's probably wise to offer him a vitamin or two each day.

Q: Is one brand of food any better than another? It seems like there are so many brands available at the pet store.

A: As a rule, if you buy a premium brand, then all are about equal in quality. Even many store-bought brands are fine-quality products. As long as you avoid generic brands, feeding any brand of high-quality food should ensure proper nutrition for your kitten. Make sure your kitten is fed a diet that is specially formulated for kittens and not adult cats. Read the label to make sure the food was tested in AAFCO feeding trials. Since there are so many brands available, it is wise to consult with your kitten's veterinarian for advice. He is trained in nutrition; the part-time pet store employees don't have the knowledge of your pet or the training to make nutritional recommendations.

Q: Occasionally my kitten doesn't eat everything we offer her. Should I be concerned?

A: Kittens, like people, occasionally skip a meal or don't eat everything you offer. Assuming the kitten is not acting sick, there is no cause for alarm. Your kitten knows when it is hungry. Various things, including the amount of food in its stomach, feeding-related hormones, blood sugar and fat levels, and even the weather (cats seem to eat less in the summer heat) all determine how much your pet will eat at any given time.

Q: My veterinarian recommends dry food, yet our kitten really enjoys the canned variety. Is one form better than the next?

A: Pet food can either be dry, semimoist, or canned. Semimoist or dry food are often recommended as they cost considerably less than canned (where you pay for the can and a large amount of water) or semimoist.

While canned food does taste better and is therefore preferred by kittens, dry food may help control periodontal disease by reducing tartar build-up.

Q: My kitten doesn't eat his meals regularly. He seems to be picky, eating a lot at one meal and then refusing food at the next. Should I be concerned about this? I hope he's getting enough to eat.

A: Like some children, some kittens can be picky eaters. While most kittens eat everything in sight and still seem to be hungry, there are other kittens that are picky and almost "cat-like" in their appetites. Assuming your kitten is acting normally otherwise and is healthy, he will eat whatever his body needs to sustain itself (and even grow as well). Rest assured that not all kittens that are picky eaters will remain that way as adult cats. Even if yours does, as long as he seems healthy and is maintaining his weight there is no cause for concern. Your kitten's body will tell him when he needs to eat.

Chapter 6
Socializing Your New Kitten

- -

Correctly socializing your kitten is the most important thing you can do to prevent future behavioral problems. The most common reason for euthanasia is a behavioral problem; therefore, preventing behavioral problems is critical to decreasing the number of unwanted pets.

The socialization period (3-12 weeks of age) is the period of time early in your kitten's life when it learns to get along with other beings, including people, other species of pets, and other cats. This period is basically the time when your kitten learns that he is a kitten. The socialization period is a critical time in your kitten's life. He's going through a lot of learning, trying to adjust to his new home and to all the things out in the world. This

period is a time of trying new things, exploring the environment, learning what's safe and what's dangerous, learning the difference between good and bad behaviors, and understanding the difference between punishment and reward.

Any interactions the kitten has during this time have a profound and lasting effect on him. It is critical to maximize good experiences and minimize bad experiences. Now is the time to set boundaries, teaching the kitten what behavior is acceptable and what behavior is unacceptable.

At 5-7 weeks, the kitten approaches any warm body without fear. This is the ideal time for learning to begin, for the kitten to be exposed to as many types

---

CRYING IN THE NIGHT . . . .

Occasionally a young kitten, usually 5-12 weeks old, that is placed in a new home goes through a short period of adjustment. Often the kitten has been living with littermates and his mother and is now taken away from this safe environment, placed into a new, strange home, and is left alone at night with no warm body for comfort or snuggling. This is traumatic for the kitten and this separation anxiety is often manifested by crying the first few nights in the new home.

The worst thing you can do is to get up every time the kitten cries. Taking the kitten to bed with you or placing it in your room

---

of people (short, tall, thin, fat, old, young, black, white, etc.) as possible. It also a good idea to socialize your kitten with other animal species if possible. For example, if you think you may purchase a puppy or adult dog later, it is a good idea to introduce your new kitten to puppies and dogs at this age. Kittens socialized with other species of animals at this young age learn to accept them later in life. There are proven cases of young kittens being socialized with mice; as the kitten ages, it comes to accept the mice as a friend and not a source of food!

The eighth week of age marks the start of stable learning. Try to maximize positive experiences; any traumatic experience that occurs starting from the eighth week of life until

approximately the twelfth week can permanently affect your kitten.

By 12 weeks of age, the kitten starts to avoid interaction with species (including types of people) it hasn't had contact with during its socialization period. Positive behavior should be reinforced again at this age. If the kitten hasn't had contact with a variety of people and animals, now is the time (and possibly the last time) you can attempt socialization of these species with your new kitten.

While the 8- to 12-week period is critical in socializing your kitten, it will no doubt have some negative experiences during this time. Several of these experiences occur at the veterinarian's office. During these 8-12 weeks of age, the kitten

is even worse. Doing this will develop a habit that is hard to break as the kitten learns that whenever he cries, you respond.

To speed up the socialization process, it's best to leave the kitten alone. It's certainly okay to check on it when it starts crying just to make sure everything is O.K. If the kitten continues to whine after checking on him, do your best to ignore it and get some sleep.

Like parents with a new baby, new kitten owners should plan on missing some sleep the first week or so. Leaving the radio on or placing a blanket or hot water bottle in the cage may help but are not cure-alls.

will make two or more visits to the doctor. These visits can be traumatic and even painful due to the necessity for vaccinations. Your doctor should try and make the experience as comfortable and pleasant as possible. Praising and rewarding the kitten for good behavior at the veterinary visits can help as well. Remember that kittens can sense and react to the emotions of their owners. If you are uncomfortable at the visit, your kitten will be as well. Don't overreact to your kitten if it whines or hisses after the vaccinations. Attempts to "baby" it will only make things worse. Gentle soothing and reassurance are all that is needed. If you are uncomfortable being in the room with the kitten when the vaccinations are given, ask the doctor if you may quietly leave before the vaccinations are administered.

During this socialization period, it is critical to start introducing your kitten to as many necessary interactions as possible. For example, consider giving your kitten a bath (which can be quite a challenge), clipping its nails, picking up and handling its feet, putting the kitten on its back until it lies still, brushing its teeth, taking food and toys away from it, cleaning its ears, opening its mouth, and brushing its coat. Have your doctor show you how to perform these procedures. Your kitten needs to be tolerant of these procedures without resisting or acting aggressive. It is critical to the well-being of your pet that you can perform necessary procedures without fear of attack.

These procedures take only a few seconds each to perform and will help you bond with your new kitten. Performing these pro- cedures regularly during the 8- to 12-week critical period of socialization will help make your kitten a great cat as he matures.

Common Owner Concerns

Q: I've heard many people say the ideal time to buy a kitten is before 6 weeks of age. Others say I should wait until the kitten is several months old and has had most of his vaccinations. Is there a best time for buying a new kitten?

A: There is no right age to buy a kitten, but there are several problems that can occur if a kitten is purchased at too young or too old an age.

If the kitten is too young when purchased (under 6 weeks of age), it may not have learned what it means to be a kitten and may have trouble interacting with other cats as it ages. If purchased too old (12 weeks or later), the kitten may not have been socialized to interact properly with humans.

The environment the kitten is coming from as well as the environment you will provide are more important than an arbitrary age. Kittens that have been properly socialized by others will behave properly in your new home if you continue to work on socializing them. A kitten reared in a "kitten mill" environment with no handling or discipline is likely to have difficulty socializing, especially if he is purchased at an older age. Most doctors recommend buying a kitten between 6 and 8 weeks old. This lets you, the new owner, start training the kitten properly during its critical learning stages. It also allows you to be the one to comfort him during veterinary visits and ensures proper medical attention and immunizations without needing to depend on a third party.

Chapter 7
Selecting a Groomer

• •

Unlike dogs, most cats do not require grooming. However, long-haired cats, which can easily become matted if not brushed daily, may require regular grooming. Mats of hair are irritating to the cat, can lead to skin infections, and can become infected with maggots in outdoor cats.

If your veterinarian offers grooming services, this is the ideal place to take your kitten. You have already established a good relationship there and have developed a rapport and degree of trust with the doctor and the staff. Additionally, the doctor is available in the event that sedatives might be needed to make it easier to groom your pet (which are sometimes necessary). Also, if the groomer detects any medical problems, these can be treated that same day by your veterinarian, which saves you another trip and expense if your pet is groomed elsewhere. If you decide to have your pet groomed at the veterinary hospital, make sure you tour the grooming area and meet the groomer. As with your doctor, you need to be comfortable with the person who will be doing the grooming.

It helps if you can accustom your kitten to regular grooming. Daily brushing or combing, along with an occasional bath, and a nail trim every one to two months, will accustom the kitten to these procedures.

Selecting a groomer involves the same steps as selecting a veterinarian. Asking friends or family members for a reference is quick and easy. If your veterinarian doesn't offer grooming, he or she or the staff can be an

HOME GROOMING ....

Home grooming, including daily brushing or combing and regular trimming of kitten's nails, is a regular part of kitten care. While you can pay the veterinarian to trim the nails, it's not a hard procedure to learn and will increase the bonding between pet and owner. Have the doctor show you how on one of your visits.

There are several brands of nail trimmers you can purchase from your veterinarian or local pet store. Rescoe nail trimmers are suitable for most cats. Also be sure you purchase some type of styptic in case the nails are trimmed too short and bleed. Powders, sticks, or liquids are available.

excellent source for a referral (they may even be able to tell you who to avoid). Using the yellow pages to locate a groomer is also convenient, but may not lead you to the best groomer. Finally, locating nearby salons as you drive in your neighborhood will give you several possible choices as well.

After collecting names of possible groomers from these sources, it's time to do some investigating. Visit several of the grooming salons. Make sure you meet the actual person who will be doing the grooming. If you

pick up any bad vibes from the groomer, this is not the place to have your kitten groomed.

Inquire about vaccination protocols. Does the shop require all animals to be vaccinated? Do they verify this by asking you to bring in the vaccination records in writing or by calling your doctor to confirm the vaccinations? A grooming salon that doesn't require vaccinations should not receive as high a ranking as one that does. Many do not, and it may be hard to find one that is this stringent; once again, veterinarians who offer grooming

When you trim the nails, avoid the quick, which is the pink area of the nail representing the artery, vein, and nerve of the nail. The quick is easily seen in white nails but difficult to see in dark

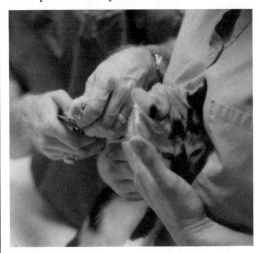

nails. As a rule, I like to leave the nails a little long so that the animal isn't "quicked" and doesn't bleed.

Brushing or combing should be done on a daily basis to remove dead hair and prevent matting of the coat. Check with your doctor or groomer for further tips on daily grooming for your pets.

All kittens should be trained to accept nail trimming.

services maintain higher standards than grooming shops. Fees are important, but less so than the feel you get for the shop and the groomer.

When leaving your kitten for grooming, make sure you and the groomer communicate clearly about what type of cut you want for your kitten. If you don't know anything about the various grooming options, ask about different clips before you ever pick a groomer. Make sure the groomer clearly explains your options and shows a willing-

ness to work with you as a first-time client.

When you pick your kitten up after its first grooming, don't panic if it looks a bit different than you expected. As with any new hair style, you never know exactly what the finished product will look like until you see it. If the kitten doesn't look quite the way you thought it would, realize that it may take a few tries for any groomer to understand your desires. Communication before and after the grooming is important so that the groomer can rectify the situation as needed.

Many groomers like to put powder in a pet's ears after bathing in an attempt to absorb excess moisture. Most veterinary dermatologists agree that powder is not needed and may increase the chance of ear infections. Ear cleaning solutions are available from your veterinarian that properly dry a pet's ear without causing ear infections. Be sure to discuss this with your veterinarian and groomer.

Finally, you may want to avoid the additional expense of a flea dip (unless the groomer sees fleas and requires it). First, many groomers use the cheapest shampoo and dip available; you may be paying for something that is ineffective. Second, if your kitten is taking ProSpot as prescribed by your doctor for flea control, it would be harmful and possibly fatal to dip the kitten.

Make sure your groomer is aware of any medical conditions your cat has to make the experience a safe one. Also, if your veterinarian recommends a certain grooming shampoo, be sure to bring that along for the groomer to use. Any groomer who refuses these requests is one to take off your list.

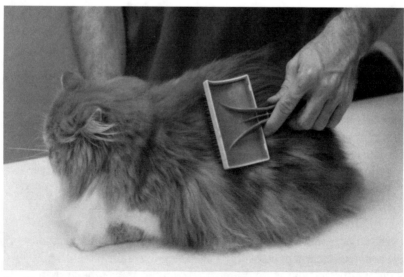

Brushing your kitten should be a part of his daily routine.

Common Owner Concerns

••

Q: Is it really necessary to pay a groomer to cut my kitten's hair? It seems like I could do it a lot cheaper.

A: It is not essential that you hire someone to clip your pet's coat. However, most owners have no formal training in grooming and don't have the time to learn or the money for the equipment, although the equipment is not expensive. If you wish to learn to groom your pet yourself, check to see if a local community college offers courses on the subject. Your pet store probably has books on grooming.

Q: Our groomer mentioned that our cat needs to be sedated the next time she comes in for grooming due to her aggressiveness. I'm concerned about tranquilizing her; is this really necessary?

A: Sedating the animal can make it easier for the groomer to do his job. It is rarely necessary, however. If a sedative needs to be given, make sure you discuss this with your cat's doctor first.

MIRACLE CURE FOR HAIR LOSS!!!!.•••••••••••••

Shedding is a normal way for pets and people to replace dead hair with new, living hair. Excessive shedding is rarely abnormal (unless there are visible bald spots) but is messy for owners to deal with. Daily brushing won't stop shedding but helps to remove a lot of the dead hair.

Some companies market various sprays that are applied to the kitten's coat on a regular basis. While some of these can help decrease shedding, they do require frequent application by the owner. Also, some owners may find the fragrance unpleasant.

A product called Prozyme, available from your doctor, may help decrease shedding in many pets. This product is an enzyme supplement placed on the pet's food. Results are seen within 2-8 weeks; most owners report little shedding while the pet is on Prozyme.

Don't let the groomer administer any medication to your pet without your doctor's OK. Teaching kittens at an early age to allow nail trimming and brushing will do a lot to prevent the need for tranquilizers at her grooming visit.

Q: The last time our cat was groomed he got a clipper burn. The groomer said it wasn't his fault, but I think he got overly aggressive with the clippers. Do I need to look for another groomer?

A: "Clipper burn" is a term used when a cat develops an area of acute moist dermatitis (a "hot spot") after grooming. The cause can be from the clippers, but more than likely there is another reason. Possibly your cat struggled during the grooming and was shaved too closely in one area.

If your cat has not been groomed in a while, the short hair produced by the recent grooming probably itched, he scratched it, it itched more, he scratched more, and he caused the abrasion or "hot spot." I wouldn't suggest switching groomers if you have not had any other problems. Make sure your cat is groomed on a regular basis as recommended by the groomer or your veterinarian. If future clipper burns occur despite regular grooming, it may be the fault of the groomer.

Chapter 8
Spaying, Neutering, or Breeding

● ●

A decision every pet owner must face is whether or not to breed or sterilize his pet. This is an important decision and it should only be made by an informed pet owner.

Breeding

There is no question that some pet owners would like to breed their cats when they get older. An important thing to consider, however, is the motivation behind the desire to breed. Three questions must be asked by every owner prior to breeding his pet:

1. Why do I want to breed my cat?
2. Should my cat be bred?
3. Can I afford to breed my cat?

Why Do I Want To Breed My Cat?

If you desire to breed your kitten when it gets older, is your motivation financial? Do you expect to make money on the kittens that result from the breeding? If money is your motivation, you should be aware that most owners who breed their cats rarely make any significant amount of money. Some owners, in fact, lose a considerable amount of money due to the cost of veterinary care for the mother and kittens and feeding the litter. Also, if you own the female cat and she has only one kitten, you are almost guaranteed not to make any money.

Do you want to breed your cat so your children can learn about the "birds and the bees"? Cats rarely give birth at a convenient time; most children aren't awake at two in the morning. How will your children act when they see the blood and fluids normally passed during the birthing process? What if the mother has problems during the delivery of the kittens? Will your children be able to understand and handle the pain and trauma involved with a complicated birth? Some cats, especially first-time mothers, are nervous and easily stressed while giving birth if they have an audience. Cats, like dogs, can prolong labor until you and the kids go back to bed.

Additionally, some cats that are stressed will actually kill and eat their newborn kittens. While this behavior is a remnant of the behavior cats exhibit in the wild, this can be traumatic for children and adults alike. Most children can learn about the birthing experience through better means than watching their cat deliver kittens.

Also keep in mind that if you own the male cat, you may have to put up with the disgusting habit of urine spraying. Male cats that are not neutered commonly spray urine as a way of marking their territories. If you maintain an intact male cat to be used for breeding, expect him to spray urine in your house!

BEFORE YOU BREED YOUR PET . . . .

If, after careful consideration, you have decided to breed your kitten when he or she reaches breeding age (2-5 years of age is preferred by many veterinarians), consider the following points before firmly committing to this project:

•• ➡ Is your pet healthy? Only healthy male or female cats should be bred. A veterinary visit prior to breeding is essential. Of course, your pet should be current on all vaccinations, be dewormed as needed, be free of internal and external parasites, and take a heart-worm preventative medication (if indicated).

•• ➡ Does your pet have any hereditary defects? Any pet with a condition which is known or suspected to be hereditary in nature

Should My Cat Be Bred?
Most pets are not the ideal standards of the breed. Some pets have medical or behavioral problems that might be passed to the offspring. Most breeders will not allow their cats to breed with a family pet, even if it is purebred, unless it is a champion and has won many contests. There are enough unwanted pets in the world; unless you cat is a *perfect* specimen (which is rare), you should not breed him or her. If you feel that your cat is a perfect specimen, consult with your veterinarian to make sure it does not have any medical or congenital problems, such as heart defects or cryptorchidism. A visit with a local breeder will confirm if your kitten is an outstanding representative of the breed.

Can I Afford to Breed My Cat?
Assuming there are no medical problems with the mother, the birthing process, or the kittens, the *minimum* cost for providing veterinary care for a female cat and an average litter of four kittens that will be sold at eight weeks of age is approximately $200. If the mother needs a Caesarean section in order to deliver the kittens, add another $300-$700 to that cost. For each sick kitten, add another $500 or so. Since most owners will get no more than $150-$250 per kitten, you can see that breeding cats is usually not a money-making business. Unless you can

---

should not be bred. These include but are not limited to atopic or allergic dermatitis, monorchism, hernias, eye defects, and heart conditions.

•• ➡ Is the owner of the intended mate responsible? Even though you may not own both the male and female, you still have a responsibility to make sure the mate for your cat is healthy and free of hereditary defects.

•• ➡ What is the cat's behavior? Only well-mannered and even-tempered pets should be used for breeding.

•• ➡ Can you keep the litter of kittens if for some reason you are unable to sell them? If you answer "no," then you should not breed your cat.

commit to providing all the care an expectant mother and new kittens will require, seriously reconsider the idea of breeding your pet. Will you be able to provide care for a litter of kittens if you have trouble finding homes? Even though you may think your kittens are cute and adorable, it doesn't mean you'll have buyers knocking down your door to take them. Kittens that are born with any problems will be harder to place.

Reasons Not to Breed Your Cat

In addition to all of the above arguments against breeding your male or female cat, there are medical and behavioral reasons for spaying or neutering.

Malignant breast cancer occurs in about one in four unspayed female dogs, compared to a one-in-nine chance in women. While we don't have exact information on the incidence of breast cancer in cats, it's probably safe to assume that it's similar to dogs. We do know that while breast tumors in dogs are only cancerous 50 percent of the time, these tumors are cancerous about 90 percent of the time in cats. The older the cat is when she is spayed, the greater the

chance of breast cancer. Kittens spayed before their first heat, which occurs at approximately six months of age, have almost no chance of developing breast cancer. After two years of age, cats should still be spayed if this has not already been done, but there is no protective effect against developing breast cancer. Nevertheless, all cats should eventually be spayed, even those that have kittens, to prevent the development of a common condition called pyometra, which is an infection (often life-threatening) of the uterus. This condition commonly develops in cats that have never been spayed; while it usually occurs in older cats past eight years of age, it can occur at any time in any unspayed female cat.

During the spaying operation, the ovaries and the uterus are removed. Cats that have been spayed will never come into heat and display the behaviors associated with the fluctuating hormone levels of intact female cats.

Neutering of male cats includes removal of the testicles and the vas deferens (spermatic cord). This prevents the hormonal effects seen in intact male cats, including urine spraying, which commonly occurs in intact male cats past the age of puberty (roughly six months of age).

While most female cats are spayed, many male cats are not neutered. This is often due to a "castration complex" among male owners. Often the wife wants the cat neutered but the husband does not. It seems that, consciously or subconsciously, the husband identifies with the cat and equates the neutering with his own castration, which somehow lowers his masculinity. Careful discussion between both husband and wife and veterinarian can usually make the neutering process less traumatic for male pet owners. While the castration complex is more common among dog owners, some cat owners also exhibit this condition.

Another reason some male cats are not neutered is because the owners have decided to make these cats "outdoor" pets. These intact male cats live outside but "come home" to eat and visit the owner. Ideally, no cat should be an outdoor cat. Outdoor pets are more prone to injury and illness and are an imposition on neighbors who may not be cat lovers. The incidence of trauma from vehicular accidents and gun shots increases as cats are left as

outdoor pets. Also, outdoor cats have a much higher incidence of diseases, including cat bite abscesses (with secondary FIV or cat AIDS infections), cat leukemia virus infections, and feline infectious peritonitis. Through the use of vaccinations, the incidences of some of these diseases has decreased sharply. However, keeping cats indoors will prevent most diseases. If for some reason your male cat prefers the outdoors, make sure he is neutered. This will prevent the fathering of unwanted kittens and decrease his desire to fight other males; cat fights often result in abscesses (which can be fatal) and the forementioned FIV infection (which is fatal).

Many owners incorrectly assume that spays and neuters are routine procedures. This is a very dangerous assumption that leads to complacency among owners and sometimes even veterinarians. Spaying and neutering are major surgical procedures. Anytime a pet is anesthetized, there is a risk of injury or even death.

The following description will help you understand what actually occurs during a spaying (ovariohysterectomy) or neutering (orchidectomy) procedure. Since your veterinarian may do things slightly differently, make sure you talk with him about the specifics of the procedure that he performs. This is definitely one time when you need to be comfortable with your choice in doctors. Do not send your pet to the lowest bidder for surgery!

1. Prior to the anesthetic, the cat is given a complete physical examination and blood tests to make sure it is healthy. Any abnormalities noted on the examination or blood tests may warrant further investigation of the problem and delay the spaying or neutering. Problems very rarely are found, but anything that might contribute to the injury or death of your pet needs to be checked out *before* an elective surgical procedure.

2. Assuming the examination and blood tests are normal, the pet will be given a sedative and usually a drug that can prevent unnecessary slowing of the heart once anesthetized. The sedative helps calm the pet and make induction of anesthesia easier. Sedatives also reduce the amount of anesthetic needed; this is wise, as the major risk involved in surgery is with the

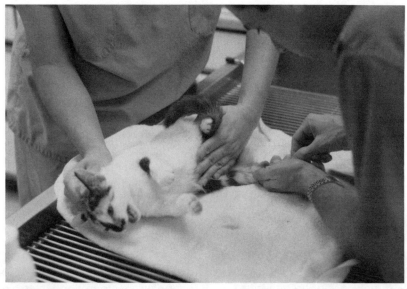

A cat is given blood tests and a complete physical examination prior to any anesthesia to make sure it is healthy.

anesthesia. Sedatives also help the pet wake up smoothly from the anesthetic and may offer some postoperative pain relief.

3. The animal can be given any of several types of anesthetic. The most expensive, but also the safest, is a gas called isoflurane. Many doctors prefer this anesthetic, as the pet's depth of anesthesia can be easily regulated. Pets that become "light" (start to wake up) can be given more gas; pets that breathe a little too slowly (become too deeply anesthetized) can be given less anesthesia. Animals are usually induced with a short-acting injectable anesthetic that allows the doctor to place a tube into its trachea (windpipe) to administer the anesthetic gas. In an attempt to cut costs, lower-priced spay and neuter clinics usually will not use isoflurane gas but opt instead for the much less expensive injectable anesthetics. These injectable anesthetics, while often safe, are not as safe as isoflurane, and the depth of anesthesia is not easily controlled. Additionally, they often wear off before the procedure ends, causing the animal to

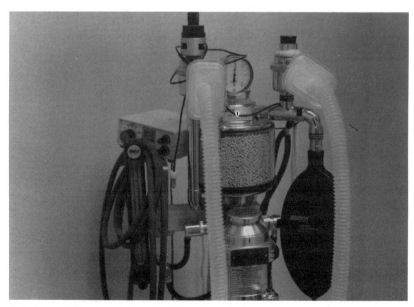

A modern anesthetic machine used for delivering isoflurane gas anesthesia during surgery. Notice the respiratory monitor (small box on the left side of the machine) which alerts the doctor of breathing pattern changes during the surgery.

feel pain from the surgery.
Finally, pets given only injectable anesthetics often wake up
violently and appear drugged or
"spaced out" for several hours
or days after the surgery.
4. The anesthesia and surgery
are monitored by a veterinary
assistant and any of several
machines. The machine could be
a respiratory monitor, which indicates when the animal breathes,
a heart monitor, which indicates
heart rate, or a new device called
a pulse oximeter which indicates
oxygen saturation of the pet's tissues. Any of these devices,

accompanied by the watchful
eye of the assistant, ensure
proper anesthetic depth and can
alert the doctor if any problems
develop during the surgical
procedure.
5. During a spay procedure,
the ovaries and uterus are
located, clamped, and tied with
absorbable suture material that
will dissolve within one to two
months. The abdomen is sutured,
usually with absorbable suture;
the skin is sutured with buried
(hidden) absorbable suture or
visible nonabsorbable suture or
stainless steel that must be

STERILIZATION AND PET BEHAVIOR . . . .

Many owners are concerned about the behavioral changes seen in
their pets after sterilization. Most of the time there will be no
changes, as far as a calming effect. Remember, these surgeries
occur when the pet is still a young kitten. Surgical sterilization
does not change that fact, and these kittens will still be energetic
and kitten-like for a long time. About 50 percent of the time, cats
that are exhibiting undesirable behaviors may have those problems
corrected by neutering or spaying. These behaviors can include
aggression, urine marking, and the desire to roam or fight with
other cats.

Spaying or neutering is best done immediately after the last set
of vaccinations, at approximately four months of age. To prevent
problems associated with the hormonal influences seen at puberty,
it is best to have these surgeries done by six months of age. However, it is never too late to have a cat spayed or neutered, and the
procedure can also be done on older pets.

removed by the doctor within seven to ten days following the surgery.

During a neuter, the testes and spermatic cord (vas deferens) are located, clamped, and tied with absorbable suture material. The skin is not usually sutured in cats but rather heals nicely as an open incision.

6. After the procedure is completed, the gas anesthetic is turned off and the animal recovers in a quiet compartment or run. The animal is usually kept overnight (at least for the spaying procedure) to ensure a quiet recovery.

As you can see, these surgeries, while common procedures, are *not* routine, and problems, though extremely rare, can arise. Make sure you are comfortable with the doctor you select to perform either of these operations on your kitten. Don't be afraid to inquire as to the exact specifics of the procedure, type of anesthesia used, type of monitoring done during the surgery, and any other questions you may have.

Aftercare of the pet is extremely important. Your doctor should review discharge instructions with you. The pet must be kept quiet; this means physical activity must be kept to

OVARIAN REMNANT SYNDROME. . . . .

Occasionally a spayed cat will still go through a heat cycle. Assuming the operation was performed correctly, the most common cause of this problem is ovarian remnant syndrome.

During the spaying procedure, the ovaries are clamped, cut, and removed, and the stump where the ovaries were attached is tied with suture material. While this is usually a straightforward procedure, in rare cases there might be microscopic amounts of ovarian tissue left in the stump. If this is the case, after spaying, that microscopic tissue will enlarge and function as another ovary.

The solution is simply to do an exploratory surgery and remove any remaining ovarian tissue; the doctor may want to send this tissue off for a biopsy to confirm that it is ovarian tissue and make sure no cancer is involved.

THE TRUE COST OF A SPAY . . . .

The next time you question why your veterinarian charges "so much" for a spay, consider the following:

Receptionist Time:
Make appt., answer questions	15 min.
Admit pet, make record	10 min.
Discharge pet	10 min.
Total time	35 min.

Total Cost (at $6/hr) $ 3.50

Technician Time:
Record keeping	10 min.
Presurgical lab tests	10 min.
Surgery Prep	10 min.
Anesthetic monitoring	30 min.
Sterilize pack, clean surgery suit	20 min.
Total time	80 min.

Total Cost (at $10/hr) $ 13.60

Cost of Anesthesia	$ 8.00
Cost of Feeding and Hospitalization	$ 5.00
Cost of Surgical Materials	$ 10.00
Overhead Costs	$ 20.00
Veterinarian's Time (at $120/hr)	$ 60.00
Total Cost	$120.10

---

a minimum (no running, jumping, or hard play) to prevent dehiscence. Dehiscence occurs when excess pressure or tension is put on the suture line; if this occurs, the wound dehisces, or breaks open, and must be resutured. This is a serious complication; wounds that break open are susceptible to infection.

These figures are average figures based on a 30 minute spay for a 10 pound cat. Charges will vary based on area of the country, length of surgery time, complications, and weight of the pet
Of course, some veterinarians charge less, often much less. Any discounted service means that something was "left out" in order for the price to be decreased. If calling around to find out the cost of a spay or neuter, make sure you know what was left out in order to save you a few dollars. Don't sacrifice quality just to save a little. Remember, spays and neuters are not "routine" procedures but rather major operations. In deciding where to take your kitten for this major surgery, ask yourself, "Would I want surgery on myself performed by the lowest bidder?" As a rule, good care isn't cheap and cheap care isn't good.

Additionally, abdominal contents, such as fat (usually) or intestines (rarely) can hang out of the open incision and can result in infection, shock, or even death if not treated immediately. If you have trouble keeping your pet quiet at home, consult with the doctor for advice. Some kittens, being active and playful, may need to be sedated until the sutures are removed. Others should be boarded for a week or confined to a cage at home during this recovery time.

While neutering and spaying can prevent urine spraying in most cats (regardless of the age of the cat when the surgery is performed), some spayed and neutered cats will spray urine in times of stress. Behavior therapy (and sometimes drug therapy) will usually control the problem (urine spraying is discussed in greater depths in Chapter 9).

Common Owner Concerns

Q: I've been told that all female cats need to go through at least one heat or even be bred prior to being spayed.

Shouldn't I wait until my cat has a litter of kittens before spaying her?

A: At one time, the general consensus was that all female cats should go through at least one heat period prior to spaying. Some doctors even recommended letting a cat have at least one litter before spaying. Now we know the many benefits of early spaying, including the significant reduction in breast cancer in cats that are spayed before their first heat. While some people still believe the old school of thought, realize that there are no benefits to putting off spaying your cat. Unless your cat is a registered champion and you have the patience and finances to handle the breeding and raising of kittens, get your kitten spayed between four and six months of age.

Q: Is the heat cycle in cats the same as the menstrual cycle in women? My cat's heat seems to be shorter than the typical period in women.

A: The heat cycle in cats is very different from the menstrual cycle in women. Cats are considered seasonally polyestrus, which means that as daylight increases (in the spring and summer), their reproductive organs become active and they begin cycling. Cats that live in more temperate climates may experience heat cycles year round. Most cats have a heat cycle every 21-30 days during their period of reproductive organ activity each year, versus approximately one menstrual cycle each month in women. For cats that show seasonal polyestrus behavior, their reproductive tracts are "quiet" or less active when compared to people.

With women, bleeding occurs as the menstrual cycle is ending, after the uterus, primed under hormonal influence for possible pregnancy, sheds its blood-rich lining.

In cats, bleeding does not usually occur. If it is seen, it occurs before the uterus is prepared for pregnancy, and indicates the start of the heat cycle. Cats, unlike dogs, people, and most mammals but similar to ferrets, rabbits, and camels, do not ovulate unless bred. They will "go out of heat" within a few days of starting their cycle, but unless bred ovulation does not occur. If needed your veterinarian can artificially stimulate your cat to ovulate so that she will end her period of estrus. While a cat is "in heat," she may become more affectionate, crouch down in front of you and present her hindquarters, and often exhibits loud vocalizations. For first time owners, these vocalizations are disturbing and seem to indicate the cat is in extreme pain or discomfort. However, this is not the case but is just a normal sign that your female cat is in heat. These behavioral changes seen with the heat cycles are further reasons to spay your kitten before puberty. As with women, these are textbook numbers for the average cat; your pet may differ without being abnormal.

Chapter 9

Common Kitten Behavior Problems

• •

Unlike puppies, kittens rarely have behavior problems. The most annoying problem owners of kittens experience is the kitten's interest in scratching everything, including the owner! The most common behavioral problems that occur in adult cats are inappropriate elimination and spraying of urine; these will be briefly discussed after the section on scratching problems in kittens.

The difficult thing for owners to understand is that most behavior problems are not necessarily abnormal behaviors. An example of an abnormal behavior would be a cat acting self-destructively, such as constantly chewing at a spot on its leg until the spot becomes raw. Most of the behav-

ior problems owners notice in their kittens are normal behaviors for the kitten, just not appreciated or allowed by owners. Like it or not, a kitten that is eliminating throughout the house or chewing furniture is engaging in normal, although unacceptable, behavior.

There are several rules to follow when attempting to ensure proper behavior in a kitten or cat, and adhering to these rules will go a long way in decreasing the time it takes to properly train your new friend.

Rule 1. It is better to praise than punish. Kittens, like people, learn more with praise than with punishment. This is not to suggest that kittens should never be punished, only that if owners have a choice, praise is always preferred.

Rule 2. In order for punishment to work, it must be initiated promptly, it must "fit the crime," and it should be of sufficient duration to correct the behavior. Punishment that lasts for too short a period is ineffective; punishment that lasts too long is cruel and also ineffective.

Prompt punishment means that the kitten must be caught "in the act" or within 30 seconds of the act. This is impossible for most owners. Often the kitten has an accident out of the owner's sight; punishment of the inappropriate elimination then is ineffective. Taking a kitten over to the spot, scolding, hitting, and rubbing the nose of the kitten in the area will *not* correct the problem but in fact will encourage the behavior and make the problem worse.

Rule 3. Finally, keep in mind that unlike puppies, kittens by nature have a different social structure than people and dogs. Their social behavior is extremely complex and not always easy to interpret. Because of this different social structure, punishment does not mean as

much to the kitten (and is less likely to work) as it would to a puppy. This is frustrating to owners and means that it is more difficult to train kittens when compared with puppies.

Scratching

It is perfectly normal for kittens to scratch. Cats and kittens use their claws when playing, when acting aggressively, when acting defensively, and as a marking behavior. In the wild, cats scratch objects such as trees not only to sharpen their claws (and remove excess dead claw material) but as a visual signal to other cats.

Kittens scratch for the same reasons, and also because they are learning different behaviors that require their claws. Thus, it is perfectly normal (although obviously frustrating and often painful to owners) when a kitten does what comes normal to it, which is to scratch everything in sight (mainly vertical objects, including owners).

There are several solutions for this problem. Obviously, declawing is the recommended permanent treatment most owners choose. Usually just the front claws are removed. This allows the rear claws to be maintained for protection in the event that the kitten would ever get outside the protective environment of the house. (The declawing procedure is discussed in detail below.) In the event that owners find it necessary to have the rear claws removed, this can be done at a later age. However, it is imperative that the cat not ever be allowed to go outdoors, as they will have a decreased chance of defending themselves.

One of the concerns among owners who consider declawing their kittens is that the cats may later become aggressive and begin biting since the cats no longer have their claws. Several studies have shown no increase in behavioral problems (including biting) in cats that are declawed. Most owners reported improvement in their relationships with their cats after declawing.

Of course, kittens are not usually declawed until four to six months of age. Until that time, owners can minimize damage to themselves and their furniture by clipping the nails as often as needed. While this will not deter scratching, it will minimize damage caused by the sharp claws. Owners can also try things such

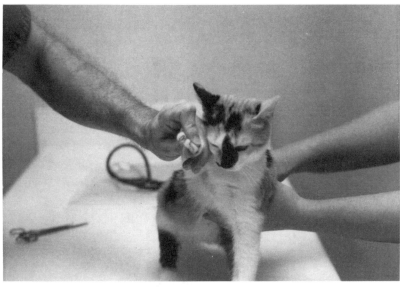

Kittens are not usually declawed until 4-6 months of age. Usually just the front claws are removed. The rear claws are left to protect the kitten in the event the kitten ever got outside the protective environment of the house.

as introducing the kitten to a scratching post and using plastic covers on furniture until the declawing operation can be performed. Regarding the scratching post, most kittens and cats seem to prefer a longitudinal orientation of the weave of the fabric. The post should be stable and tall, at least twelve inches in height. Additionally, post usage can be encouraged by placing a favorite toy on top of the post and, if needed, placing the kitten and the post in a room where the post is the only piece of furniture.

Declawing

There are many myths about declawing that are propagated by those who are adamantly opposed to this procedure. Obviously, the procedure serves no real medical purpose other than to prevent or treat unacceptable clawing behavior by the cat or kitten. The procedure is most easily performed on young kittens as the extensor ligaments are not fully developed at this age. The declawing is performed under general anesthesia, and a pain killing medication can be given if needed. There are two different procedures that can be performed to remove the claw. In one procedure, the claw is

separated from the bone to which it attaches. While there is nothing wrong with this procedure, because the bone and the claw are not removed there is always the slight chance that the claw can regrow if the germinal tissue (from which the claw originates) is not removed.

I routinely perform a variation of this procedure in which I remove the claw and the last bone to which the claw is attached. This ensures that the claw cannot regrow.

After removing the claw, surgical glue is applied to the open wounds and then the feet are bandaged for 24 to 48 hours.

Most of the time there are no postoperative complications. Rarely, one of the surgical wounds can become infected. For this reason, I instruct owners to use a special litter (I prefer Yesterday's News, a recycled newspaper litter) that is less likely to find its way into the surgical incisions. A small amount of postoperative lameness (mild limping) may also be seen.

Those opposed to declawing compare it to removing a person's fingers. Keep in mind, however, that kittens do not have fingers, so the comparison is not accurate. The procedure is not cruel or painful if done properly and if pain-killing medication is used. In many cases owners cannot live with a cat which is destroying furniture and wallpaper or constantly scratching the owner. Often declawing is their last hope or the cat would be given away or euthanized. Because inappropriate scratching is one of the few behavior problems that we can cure, declawing should be viewed as a safe and painless procedure that can make many cats acceptable pets for their owners.

Inappropriate Elimination

Owners commonly have concerns about elimination problems in their kittens. Inappropriate elimination can involve urine or feces or both, although most commonly inappropriate urination is the major complaint. When discussing elimination, it is important to differentiate between elimination and urine marking or spraying. This is important because the causes and treatments of the two problems are different.

Inappropriate Urination has many causes. For cats and kittens that urinate outside of the litterbox, owners should keep the following points in mind:

•• ➡ Make sure the litterbox is clean. Some kittens are so tidy that the box needs to be changed after every elimination.

•• ➡ Make sure the kitten can enter the box. The box should be easy to use; if the walls are too high, the kitten may not be able to comfortably enter the box to eliminate.

•• ➡ Change types of litter slowly if you need to change them. Some kittens definitely prefer one type of litter over another.

•• ➡ Supply an ample number of litterboxes. As a rule for homes with more than one cat, provide one more box than the number of cats in the house (if you have two cats, provide three boxes).

•• ➡ If the kitten prefers to urinate in one special spot, often another litterbox or the food or water bowl placed over the spot will correct the behavior. And when cleaning the spot, remember not to use products that contain ammonia, as ammonia smells similar to urine as far as cats are concerned.

Urine Spraying or Marking is a common problem in cats. It most often occurs in intact (non-neutered) males; however, most owners are surprised to hear that *any* cat can spray urine. Cats usually do not spray urine unless they are stressed; therefore, whenever a cat begins spraying urine it is important to determine *why* the cat has begun this habit. In other words, what stress caused the cat to begin spraying urine? It may be that another cat was brought into the house, or maybe the owner moved to a new house. Usually, the stress can be identified.

Sometimes it is difficult to determine if the cat is urinating inappropriately or if urine spraying is occurring. As a rule, cats that spray urine mark vertical objects with urine; those that urinate outside of the box usually urinate on a horizontal object such as the floor. If the owner actually watches the cat in the act, those that spray usually stand, hold the tail vertically, and spray the object. Cats that urinate outside of the litterbox assume a normal urinating (squatting) position.

Treatment of urine spraying/marking involves behavior modification and often mood-altering drugs to reduce the anxiety of the cat. Regardless of the cause, the cat's stress (or its perceived stress) must be reduced or eliminated. There is no magic pill. The sooner the problem is addressed the greater the chance of success. Treatment and cure do not happen overnight; owners must be patient and be committed to the pet's treatment.

Early neutering (and spaying) will usually (but not always) prevent urine spraying. However, even adult cats that spray can often be cured by neutering or spaying regardless of age. Surgical sterilization is the recommended treatment for intact cats that develop urine spraying. If this is not effective, then behavior therapy and/or drug therapy may be indicated in order to reduce the cat's stress.

Chapter 10
Common Diseases

. . . .

While preventing illness is every owner's goal, your kitten may require veterinary attention for an illness at some point in its life. Most kittenhood illnesses are mild and not life-threatening, as is true of many childhood diseases. Early diagnosis and treatment are important in help-ing your kitten make a quick and smooth recovery. Illness is hard on kittens; the sooner they recover from an illness, the happier you both will feel.

This section talks about some of the most common conditions affecting kittens.

Cardiomyopathy
. . . .

Cardiomyopathy indicates a diseased condition of the cardiac or heart muscle. It is probably the most common condition of adult cats. Heart disease is rare in kittens but can occur as a result of congenital developmental abnormalities. For example, in the developing fetus, the heart valves may not form properly, or the chambers may not develop as they should. Heart disease in kittens is usually detected during one of the kitten visits. Many owners question why kittens need to see the veterinarian so often, and owners also question why the doctor needs to perform a complete physical examination during each visit. It's possible that a problem exists that may not appear on every visit. By performing repeated examinations, the chance of detecting a problem is increased. Since it's much better for the pet to detect a problem before the kitten acts sick, the repeated physical examinations are in your kitten's best interests.

Cardiomyopathy, a common heart disease in cats, most commonly occurs in young cats, particularly male cats. This is different from the condition in dogs, in which heart diseases usually occur in older, small breeds of dogs. There are several types of cardiomyopathy. One type, called dilated cardiomyopathy, rarely occurs anymore. That's because it was discovered that this type of heart disease is most commonly associated with the deficiency of taurine, an essential amino acid in cats. Since this discovery, all cat food companies have increased the supplementation of taurine in their foods. Cats that are diagnosed with the dilated form of cardiomyopathy often respond to taurine therapy. In the past, this type of cardiomyopathy was usually fatal. Thanks to the discovery of taurine deficiency, when diagnosed early, this form of heart disease is rarely fatal now.

The most common form of cardiomyopathy is called hypertrophic cardiomyopathy. This form is not related to the deficiency of taurine or any other nutrients in the cat's food. Unlike dilated cardiomyopathy, where the heart wall becomes very thin, the heart chambers dilate, and the heart loses its strength and can't pump blood effectively, in hypertrophic cardiomyopathy the heart walls become severely thickened. This thickening, which occurs on the inside of the heart, causes the heart chambers to shrink in size. This means that there is less room for blood in the heart chambers and less blood to supply the body with the oxygen which it requires.

So how is cardiomyopathy diagnosed? Ideally, and most commonly, an abnormal heart sound (either a heart murmur, caused by turbulent blood flow in the heart, or a gallop rhythm, caused by abnormal extra heart beats) is heard during a routine physical examination. Most of the times these cats are asymptomatic, which means that the cat is not showing any signs of heart disease. This is the ideal time to diagnose this condition, since the cat is not in heart failure at this time. Diagnosing cardiomyopathy in a cat which is not showing signs of heart disease is also the least expensive time for owners, as it is always less expensive to diagnose and treat a pet that appears healthy than when it is ill.

After the abnormal heart sounds are detected, the doctor will probably recommend a variety of tests to determine just how

WHEN TO CALL THE DOCTOR. . . . .

As a new kitten owner, you probably worry at the slightest thing that seems wrong. Don't feel bad; you're not alone. The following information may help you know when to call the doctor.

What's normal:
- An occasional sneeze
- An occasional cough
- One episode of vomiting or diarrhea, *if* no blood is seen and the kitten acts normal
- Short bouts of hiccups
- Mild shaking when asleep
- One skipped meal if the kitten seems normal otherwise
- A small amount of *clear* discharge from the eyes if the eyes are not red
- An occasional itch

What's not. . . (Call your veterinarian **immediately**!):
- A kitten that's sluggish, slow to wake up, or lethargic
- A kitten that shows no interest in several types of food —canned, dry, human baby food
- Red eyes, closed eyes, any eye discharge that is not clear
- Excessive scratching
- Shaking the head excessively
- More than one bout of vomiting or diarrhea
- Blood in the vomit or stool
- Abnormal size or shape to the abdomen
- Rapid breathing or difficulty breathing
- Tumors, lumps, or bumps seen or felt on the kitten
- Blood coming from any body opening

advanced the heart disease is. Tests such as blood tests, a urinalysis, radiographs of the chest (X-rays), and an ultrasound examination of the heart are needed to determine if medication is needed and what the prognosis for the cat is.

Most cats that are diagnosed and treated at an early stage of the disease will live a long, healthy life. Many of these cats are placed on low salt diets to decrease the fluid load presented to the heart. Various drugs may be prescribed to lower the heart rate; often in mild forms of cardiomyopathy, early treatment may actually correct the heart condition. If abnormal heart beats (arrythmias) are present, drugs are prescribed to control these.

Aspirin is often prescribed for cats diagnosed with heart disease. A side effect of cardiomyopathy is the formation of a blood clot in the heart. This clot, called a thrombus, can break loose and become an embolus, spreading to other parts of the body. Most commonly the embolus lodges in the aorta, the large blood vessel leading from the heart to the rest of the body. The embolus usually gets stuck at the end of the aorta where the aorta gives off other vessels that supply blood to the rear legs. Cats

with an embolus from cardiomyopathy are often seen for paralysis in the rear legs. While there is no definitive evidence that aspirin use can prevent the thrombus formation and subsequent embolization of the aorta, most doctors still recommend it in the hopes that thrombus formation may be decreased. One word of warning: because aspirin can be very toxic to cats, *never* use aspirin without a doctor's recommendation.

Fortunately, most cats that are diagnosed and treated early do very well. It is often difficult to convince owners to spend the money necessary to run the diagnostic tests and start treatment for cardiomyopathy. Cats that do not receive the diagnostic tests and treatment will eventually progress to full blown heart failure; some may even experience sudden death from embolus formation. There is no way to know how long a cat which receives the diagnosis of cardiomyopathy but which does not receive diagnostic testing and treatment will live. Therefore, it is very important to allow the doctor to perform the tests he recommends. If you have been wise enough to purchase health insurance for your pet, then the costs of the tests are very reasonable.

FIRST AID AND EMERGENCY KIT . . . .

It's often convenient to have a small first-aid kit available for
minor problems. You can make one yourself and store the supplies
in a fishing tackle box, or buy one already assembled at the drug-
store.

In all honesty, in a true emergency there is very little any pet
owner can do at home other than stop major bleeding, assist in
breathing, and get the kitten to the doctor as soon as possible. For
minor problems, the following information can assist you.

Bleeding   Stop the bleeding. For cut nails, use styptic powder
or liquid, corn starch or flour, or bar soap. Never trim nails unless
you have some type of styptic. Make sure your doctor shows you
the proper way to trim nails. In general, if the bleeding doesn't
stop within ten minutes, see your veterinarian.

For more serious bleeding from cuts, direct pressure on the
bleeding area for five to ten minutes should stop the bleeding.
Large gashes may require suturing and should be seen to by the
veterinarian. You can bandage minor wounds, although bandaging
is more difficult with cats than people because of their anatomy
and the fact that many kittens will chew the bandages. If you apply
a bandage, especially on a limb, make sure it's not too tight or the
blood supply can be interrupted.

Not Breathing   If your kitten isn't breathing, prompt
veterinary attention is needed. You can blow into the nostrils while
holding the mouth closed (once every five to ten seconds). Try to
feel for a heartbeat over the chest just behind the elbows near the
breastbone. If no beat is felt, you can try CPR by laying the kitten
on its side, laying one hand on the underside of the chest and one
hand on the upper side of the chest where the heart is located, and
pressing your hands together at least one compression per second.
(You might ask your veterinarian to demonstrate this technique.)

Upper Respiratory Diseases

• •

Upper respiratory diseases are among the most common infectious diseases seen in kittens. They are usually caused by a herpes virus (called rhinotracheitis), a calici virus, or chlamydia.

These diseases are the ones that kittens receive a series of vaccinations against during their kitten visits at 8, 12, and 16 weeks of age. While chlamydial infection is not as common as rhinotracheitis or calici virus infection, some (but not all) doctors vaccinate against the disease. Because it usually doesn't add to the cost of the vaccination and will protect against another cause of respiratory disease in kittens, I recommend it as part of the kitten's vaccinations.

Kittens acquire infections by close association with infected kittens or cats. Virus is shed in nasal, oral, and ocular discharges. Objects (such as food bowls and toys) can transmit the virus if they are contaminated. Cats that recover from herpes virus stay infected (like people with herpes virus infections), remain carriers, and are capable of developing the disease later in life and intermittently shedding the virus to other cats. Cats that recover from calicivirus infection continue to shed the virus for months or years.

While there are certainly differences between each of the organisms that cause respiratory disease in kittens, the clinical signs seen with infection are similar. These can include fever, sneezing, nasal and/or ocular discharge, eye ulcers, oral ulcers, and pneumonia. Occasionally enteritis (inflammation of the intestines) and swollen and painful joints ("limping kitten syndrome") can be seen with calicivirus infection.

Diagnosis is straightforward, and although it is not always possible to tell which organism is causing the infection, this is usually not necessary since treatment is similar for all respiratory infections.

Leukemia

In people, we think of leukemia as a type of blood cancer. Normally, people with leukemia have abnormal white blood cell counts.

With cats, this is not usually the case. Many different disease manifestations can occur, including tumor formation, anemia, platelet disorders, true blood leukemia, and commonly chronic diseases such as chronic diarrhea or respiratory infections that result from a suppressed immune system. Leukemia in cats is caused by a virus, and there are several different manifestations of this disease, including cancerous and noncancerous conditions.

The virus is transmitted mainly through the saliva, although the virus is also shed in tears, milk, and urine. Close contacts between cats is necessary for the virus to spread. Having two cats in the same room does not necessarily mean danger to the non-infected cat unless intimate contact occurs. Intimate contact which allows the spread of the virus includes mutual grooming, fighting, or sharing the same food or water bowl. Additionally, transfer across the placenta and through the milk can occur in kittens born to infected mothers.

About 2-3 percent of cats in the U.S. are positive for leukemia virus; the prevalence is higher for cats between one to six years of age, and is highest in unvaccinated, outdoor cats. Susceptibility of cats to leukemia is strongly influenced by age; older cats with stronger immune systems are less likely to become and remain infected.

There is an important difference between infection and disease, not only in relation to leukemia but to any disease. A cat may become infected with leukemia but not necessarily contract the disease leukemia. It may be that the cat fights off the infection and rids its body of the leukemia virus. This happens quite often. A few cats may not fight off the infection but still not contract the disease for a long period of time.

It's important for owners to understand this, especially if their cat is diagnosed on a blood test as being positive for leukemia virus. A positive test only means that at that particular moment the cat tested positive for the disease. It does not mean that the cat will die from leukemia virus infection, and it may be a false positive, which means that the test was inaccurate (every laboratory test has a certain low rate of false positive and false negative results). For this reason, a healthy cat with a positive test should be retested in eight to twelve weeks. If the cat remains positive, an IFA test should be done to see if the infection is in the cat's bone marrow.

Leukemia infection can be prevented through vaccination. Even indoor cats should be vaccinated after receiving a negative test result. Outdoor cats should be tested annually for leukemia and feline AIDS virus infections; those that test positive should probably not receive any vaccinations except a rabies vaccine, as the cat's immune response may be diminished making vaccination ineffective.

Most cats that are not ill and test positive on several tests are persistently infected and will die of a leukemia related disease within three years of diagnosis. Sick cats can receive supportive treatment, but leukemia is considered a fatal disease.

Feline Infectious Peritonitis (FIP)

The term FIP is short for feline infectious peritonitis, a cat disease caused by a corona virus. This disease is one of the most confusing for pet owners and veterinarians. This is because the classical FIP test does *not* test for the FIP virus, but rather for any cat corona virus.

There are several strains of cat corona viruses. Some strains cause mild diarrhea, whereas others cause FIP. The test does not distinguish between which corona virus may be infecting the sick cat, only that a corona virus has infected the cat at some time and the cat has formed antibodies against the virus.

Feline infectious peritonitis usually affects outdoor cats that have a greater chance of being exposed to the virus. Infection apparently results following oral or nasal exposure. While not all infected cats will develop FIP, many will. Once clinical signs are seen, the disease is usually fatal and recovery is unlikely.

Clinical signs seen with FIP fall into two categories: a wet form and a dry form. In the wet form (which is the easiest form to diagnose), fluid accumulates (hence the term "wet form") in the chest and/or abdominal cavities as a result of blood vessel damage. Signs that can be seen include an enlarged abdomen (from the fluid accumulation), difficulty breathing (if fluid accumulates in the chest), loss of appetite, weight loss, lethargy, fever, and dehydration.

The dry form presents more difficulty in establishing a correct diagnosis. Pyogranulomatous lesions (small tumor-like nodules representing infection) can develop anywhere in the body. Signs are seen based upon what areas of the body develop the lesions. Lesions in the eye may cause blindness; lesions in the liver or kidney may cause liver or kidney failure. Sometimes lesions develop in the spinal cord and can cause a variety of neurological signs such as seizures or paralysis. Fever usually develops with this form as well.

Feline infectious peritonitis is most common in young kittens six months old to two years of age. Diagnosis of FIP is difficult. The wet form is usually easiest to diagnose since the accumulated fluid can be analyzed. Because so many diseases can mimic the dry form, diagnosis is very difficult. The only way to reach a definitive diagnosis with this form is with a biopsy, and sometimes that can only be done after the pet has expired.

We've already mentioned the antibody blood test for FIP and the problems associated with this test. A positive test only means that the kitten has been exposed to some type of corona virus at some point in its life. Also, some kittens will test positive, having been vaccinated against common kitten diseases, as a result of a cross-reaction with the components of the vaccines. Finally, it is possible for a pet to have FIP and receive a negative test result.

Of course, the test is not totally useless. If the doctor strongly suspects FIP, the kitten has signs suggestive of FIP, and the test is strongly positive, that gives support to the suspected diagnosis. Unfortunately, many doctors proclaim a cat as having FIP on the basis of one positive result of a fairly inaccurate test. This is sad, as there is no cure for FIP and it is usually fatal. The wet form is usually rapidly progressive. Treatment using corticosteroids or immunosuppressive drugs may help prolong the pet's life, but the disease is ultimately fatal for most cats.

A vaccine recently developed does seem to be effective and safe, although one early study (that has not been repeated) showed a higher incidence of FIP in vaccinated cats versus non-vaccinated cats. It will be up to each owner to decide if her cat should receive this vaccine. Cats that spend a large amount of time outdoors, especially if they live in an area with a high incidence of FIP, may benefit from the vaccine. I currently don't recommend the vaccine for patients that are indoor cats, and the incidence of the disease in my practice is extremely low (FIP is usually a sporadic disease anyway, unlike many other more common cat diseases).

Cat AIDS

The cat AIDS virus was discovered in the mid to late 1980s. In a California cattery, many cats were dying with leukemia-like diseases yet consistently tested negative on tests for the leukemia virus. Careful investigation revealed a new virus which was named the feline immunodeficiency virus (FIV). This virus is similar in many ways to the human AIDS virus; however, it does not cause AIDS in people (nor does the human virus which causes AIDS, the HIV virus, infect cats). The cat virus also is not transmitted sexually but rather through bite wounds (which means FIV infection is more common in outdoor cats, especially unneutered male cats).

FIV, like other viruses, can cause both infection and disease. Many cats will become infected but not become ill with the disease for many years (similar to HIV infection in people). Once the disease develops, it is ultimately considered a fatal condition.

Like leukemia, FIV can cause many conditions. Often cats will have chronic skin, intestinal, or respiratory infections; chronic gingivitis and periodontal disease also occur commonly. The full-blown disease (AIDS) causes fever, enlarged lymph nodes, anemia, lack of appetite, wasting, and occasionally neurological signs.

As mentioned, outdoor cats are more susceptible; infections occur in males three times as often as in females. The mean age at the time of diagnosis is about five years. Because false positive and false negative tests results can occur, a cat that tests positive should be retested. As with people infected with HIV, the Western blot test is a definitive (confirmatory) test.

Bite wounds are the most common means of infections; fetal kittens can be infected if the mother is infected during the pregnancy.

Treatment is mainly supportive; specific conditions such as diarrhea and periodontal disease should be treated specifically as needed.

There is currently no vaccine for this disease. Prevention, by testing all cats and keeping all cats indoors, is recommended. Outdoor cats should be tested for FIV and feline leukemia virus annually prior to vaccinations. Because it is questionable if infected cats can respond appropriately to vaccinations, infected cats should probably not receive annual vaccinations except for the rabies virus which is often mandated by state law.

Because leukemia and feline immunodeficiency viruses cannot be transmitted to people, there is no major public health concern. However, because these viruses induce deficient immune states, they may allow shedding of other organisms (such as toxoplasma or cryptosporidia) by the infected cat. These other conditions are transmittable to people. For this reason, it is probably safest if pregnant women, infants, the elderly, and anyone with a compromised immune system (HIV infected people, people undergoing chemotherapy) not be exposed to cats with leukemia or FIV infection.

Feline Acne

Believe it or not, cats can get acne. Unlike in people, the disease is not usually a pustular disease (no true pimples are formed). Most commonly, the cat appears to have a dirty chin. In the more sever cases, larger pustular sores are formed; these indicate infection and are painful.

The exact reason some cats develop acne is not known. It is speculated that this area may be harder for the cat to clean and therefore more prone to developing acne.

The mild form is easily treated with gentle washing with a mild soap and water, followed by a gentle swabbing of the area with alcohol. The more severe form requires antibiotics, both orally and topically. Mild acne may not always be "cured" but can usually be controlled.

Miliary Dermatitis

Miliary dermatitis is the name given to a common skin condition in cats and kittens. The name describes the lesions seen on the cat's skin but does *not* tell us what causes the lesions. The condition is called miliary dermatitis because the typical lesions, tiny crusted bumps called papules, resemble millet seed. While the term miliary dermatitis accurately describes the look and feel of the skin, it doesn't tell us what caused the cat to develop the condition.

There are many causes of miliary dermatitis, so it's not uncommon for the veterinarian to recommend a variety of tests to determine the exact cause. Common causes of miliary dermatitis include flea allergy, atopic dermatitis, food allergy, drug reaction, autoimmune diseases, sensitivity to intestinal parasites, ringworm, mange, ear mites, lice, bacterial infections, and fatty acid or other nutritional deficiencies.

Diagnostic tests your doctor may recommend include skin scrapings to check for mange mites, a fungal culture to check for ringworm, and even a skin biopsy. If an allergic reaction is suspected, your doctor may prescribe corticosteroids and watch your pet's response. If an infection is suspected, a trial dose of antibiotic therapy might be recommended. In our area of the country, a reaction to fleas is a common cause of miliary dermatitis; we often recommend aggressive fleas control as a way of diagnosing and treating these cases.

Allergic Diseases

Atopy

Atopy, also called atopic dermatitis, occurs more commonly in dogs than in cats. However, it is one of the causes of miliary dermatitis. It is usually seen in cats between six months and twenty-four months old. Atopy is often referred to as skin allergies. It is caused by the pet inhaling or absorbing foreign proteins (allergens) through its skin. The pet develops an allergic response to these allergens and signs of allergic dermatitis are then seen.

Just like people, kittens can become allergic to any number of things. Grasses, trees, house dust, pollen, and molds are most common. Many of these pets are allergic to fleas and bacteria as well. The condition is mainly seen in parts of the country where fungus and pollen counts are a problem; the only way to cure the condition is to move to a part of the country where the prevalence of allergies is low or nonexistent!

Most pets with atopic dermatitis are moderately to severely itchy. The skin lesions can resemble those of the typical cat with miliary dermatitis. Other skin reactions in cats with atopy include hair loss or eosinophilic lesions (red lesions on the body). With rare exception, most atopic pets do not have the typical respiratory signs that people with allergies exhibit, such as runny eyes or noses.

Compounding the problem of atopic dermatitis is the fact that many of these pets have coexisting conditions such as flea allergy dermatitis and skin infections. Allergic skin is more vulnerable to infections. As a matter of fact, pets with chronic skin and ear infections should be checked for atopic dermatitis to see if that is a cause of their chronic infections.

Diagnosis is usually more challenging in cats than in dogs because the disease looks different in dogs than in cats, and because cats with miliary dermatitis can have a number of causes of their skin lesions. Often pets with suspected atopic dermatitis may need to have a skin test performed to confirm the diagnosis. This painless procedure involves injecting tiny amounts of various foreign proteins (grasses, pollens, etc.) into the pet's skin and observing any hive reactions that occur. Hives that form at the spots of the injections indicate that the pet is probably allergic to that particular substance. As many as twenty-five or fifty different foreign proteins may be tested at one time; which ones your doctor chooses depends upon the time of year and what part of the country you live in.

In order to determine which allergens your cat may be sensitive to, some doctors perform a blood test in place of the standard skin test. While a blood test can sometimes be a helpful second test in questionable cases, most dermatologists agree that it is an inferior and often inaccurate test when compared with the skin test. Consult with your veterinarian to find out which test he recommends for your pet.

It should be pointed out that food allergies cannot be diagnosed by skin or blood testing, despite some claims otherwise.

In discussing allergies, it's important for owners to appreciate the summation effect. To simply explain this, let's suppose that your pet has allergies to ten different foreign proteins, such as dust, pollens, and fleas. If eight of these allergens are present at the same time, your kitten will itch and scratch himself. If only seven of these allergens are present, no itching or scratching will occur. This means that if somehow you can avoid several of these proteins, the pet will never itch even though he has allergies. While it's impossible to avoid certain trees in the area when they pollinate, you can minimize exposure to other allergens that might bother the kitten, such as fleas, feather pillows, house dust, and certain houseplants. Since cats are often allergic to ten or even twenty or more proteins, short of moving to another state, it's impossible for every owner to prevent his pet from coming in contact with many of these allergens.

Treating a pet with allergies depends upon many factors, such as the age of the pet, length of the allergy season (most pets are just allergic during certain times of the year initially, with the allergies often becoming a year-round problem as the cat ages), willingness of the owner to perform the frequent bathing and medicating usually required, and finances of the owner. While the basic treatment is similar for most allergic cats, every pet is different. Some respond well to the first antihistamine that is tried, while others fail to respond to any antihistamine and ultimately need to be skin tested and placed on desensitization therapy (allergy shots).

Corticosteroids are frequently used as an anti-itching drug for atopic dermatitis. The benefit is that most allergic cats drastically improve with corticosteroid therapy. There are some bad points to these drugs, however. Short-term side effects, which almost always occur, include excessive eating, drinking, and urinating. Rarely, some cats will become hyperactive or depressed on these drugs, although most pets show no personality change other than possibly being more energetic (this is because corticosteroids make pets "feel

good"). These short-term effects should not be of enough concern to prevent you from giving them if prescribed. Long-term side effects can include diabetes, osteoporosis, increased infections, Cushing's disease, and Addison's disease (these last two, as well as diabetes, can be serious and even life-threatening). These long-term side effects would only be seen with extremely high doses of corticosteroids, and usually only if the pet had taken them regularly for long periods of time (months to years). Most owners should not shy away from the intermittent use of low-dose corticosteroids when prescribed by the doctor. You should question the doctor, however, if long-acting depot injections are used, or if he fails to mention other, safer forms of therapy for cats with chronic allergies.

Antihistamines can also be used. Most doctors use these only when other forms of therapy fail to stop the itching or when corticosteroid use becomes excessive. There are many antihistamines, some inexpensive and some fairly costly. Be advised *never* to give your pet over-the-counter medications without instructions from your doctor. This practice can be dangerous or even fatal, especially since cats are often more sensitive to antihistamines than dogs. A common side effect from antihistamines is drowsiness. It is often necessary for the doctor to prescribe several different antihistamines as well as different dosages before finding one that works for your pet.

Fatty acid supplements can also be used. There are several prescription products available from your veterinarian. These products can work well as the only medication needed to control itching in some cats. Most cats need other medications in addition to oral fatty acids to control their allergies. The fatty acids can still help control the inflammation and itching associated with atopic dermatitis by lowering the doses of other potentially more toxic medications. For this reason, even if fatty acids don't help your pet when administered as the only medication, your doctor may still prescribe them as part of the regimen.

Prozyme is an enzyme supplement that increases the digestion and absorption of certain nutrients in the food. Some pets taking Prozyme can get relief from their allergies. As with oral fatty acids, Prozyme is often used as an adjunct to treatment rather than as the sole medication.

While most owners don't relish the thought of frequently bathing their cats, pets with allergies need frequent shampooing. Remember that many of the foreign proteins that cause your cat to itch are absorbed through his skin. Frequent shampooing decreases his exposure to the problem by removing these sources of itching. Shampooing thus serves as a type of temporary avoidance to the allergens. Most doctors prescribe a regimen of shampooing and conditioning with a medicated anti-itching shampoo and conditioner at least two to three times each week.

Some pets are so allergic that doctors suggest owners not take them outdoors for longer than necessary. Making your cat an indoor pet is a logical recommendation if he has severe allergic dermatitis and also for the other reasons already mentioned.

Food Allergy

"Food allergy" has become a catch-all term for many owners and doctors and used whenever a kitten has some sort of medical problem that resolves with a change of diet. True allergy to food is rare. The term food allergy, also called food hypersensitivity, implies that the immune system is reacting to something in the diet. A better term is food sensitivity, which implies an adverse reaction to something in the diet but which does not involve the immune system. Food sensitivities can cause reactions involving the skin (most commonly) or gastro-intestinal or respiratory systems. Food allergies account for only about 10 percent of all allergies actually diagnosed in cats and dogs. This 10 percent is the number of cases seen by veterinary dermatologists; most general practitioners feel that food-related dermatitis probably constitutes less than 1 percent of all allergic dermatitis.

While a few cats with food sensitivities will suffer gastrointestinal disturbances such as vomiting and diarrhea, the most frequent sign is severe itching anywhere on the body, most commonly around the head.

Contrary to what most owners think, pets that are vulnerable to food sensitivities usually develop that sensitivity to a diet they have been eating for a substantial length of time, often well over two years! It would be extremely rare for a pet to develop a true sensitivity to a food that it has been consuming for only a short period of time, although certainly problems, such as vomiting or diarrhea, can develop when a new food is offered, especially if the new diet was introduced suddenly rather than gradually.

When we speak of a food sensitivity or hypersensitivity, we're actually talking about a pet becoming sensitized to certain ingredients in the food, rather than the entire diet itself. Remember that pet food is composed of many ingredients; sensitivities can develop to any of these ingredients. Because proteins are mostly "antigenic," the protein sources in the food are most likely to cause a problem. These protein sources can include any type of meat, including beef, chicken, pork, and yes, even lamb! Other sources that can cause a problem include milk, eggs, wheat, oats, horse meat, cornmeal, and yeasts. In cats, fish and dairy products are most often blamed. Food additives account for only about 5 percent of food sensitivities; this means that buying "additive-free" foods does little to help control food sensitivities. However, the increased use of

TOXOPLASMOSIS ....

Toxoplasmosis is a protozoan disease that can affect cats. It is the disease that is often discussed among pregnant women as a cause of concern since toxoplasma organisms can infect people and cause damage (or death) to the fetus.

There is a lot of misinformation about this disease. Often, the woman's obstetrician will recommend getting rid of the cat because of the potential threat to the developing baby. This recommendation is unfounded and not necessary if the woman will follow some common-sense guidelines while keeping the following facts in mind.

●●➡ While you can contract toxoplasmosis from the pet cat, you are more likely to get it from eating rare or raw meat or raw vegetables that have not been thoroughly cleaned.

●●➡ Indoor cats won't acquire the organism unless they are exposed to another cat's feces or eat an infected mouse or rat, both of which are unlikely.

●●➡ When a cat contracts toxoplasma organisms, it will then shed the organisms in its feces for about two to three weeks until its body produces antibodies against the toxoplasma organisms. Once the cat forms antibodies, the shedding of infected organisms in the feces stops. Rarely, if a cat develops an immunosuppressive disease (such as leukemia or cancer) or becomes pregnant, it may shed organisms in the future. For most cats, once they have developed antibodies they will never be able to infect other cats or people again. Simply put, most owners' cats are only able to infect them for two to three weeks out of the cat's entire life if even that.

Occasionally, a client comes in on the advice of her obstetrician wanting us to test her cat for toxoplasmosis. Some clients want us to check the cat's feces. However, since a cat only sheds the organisms in its feces for two to three weeks out of its entire life, there's not much chance of finding organisms in a random fecal sample (unlike the case with other intestinal parasites).

A blood test can be done on the cat, but results can be confusing. A cat that tests positive is actually a safer cat to have, since a positive test indicates that the cat is making antibodies to the disease and is unlikely to shed the organism. A cat that tests negative is potentially infective to the owner.

A blood test on the pregnant woman may be the best idea. Many people in our country have toxoplasma organisms in their body due to contracting the organism from cat exposure or from eating habits. Obviously, while many people have the organism without even knowing it, most of us will never develop the disease toxoplasmosis.

To prevent the chance of contracting toxoplasmosis, here are a few tips to follow:

••➡ Don't eat undercooked meat.

••➡ If you eat raw vegetables, make sure they are thoroughly cleaned.

••➡ If you garden, wear gloves.

••➡ Do not let your cat run loose outdoors.

••➡ Don't handle cats other than your own.

••➡ Don't get a new kitten or cat while you are pregnant.

••➡ Have your spouse change the litterbox daily (it takes two to three days for the organisms in the feces to develop to the infective stage).

additive-free foods has increased the incidence of food poisoning in pets. Food processing can make a food more or less likely to cause a reaction in cats. Because a sensitivity to ingredients in the food often takes a year or more to develop, food sensitivities and hypersensitivities are problems that are not encountered in most kittens.

Owners are often surprised to hear that a pet can develop a food sensitivity to lamb and rice diets. Many manufacturers advertise lamb and rice diets as being hypoallergenic, and sales of these premium diets have skyrocketed in recent years. Unfortunately, all of the advertising is just hype to get you to buy these more expensive diets. There is nothing inherently "hypoallergenic" about lamb. The reason most pets are not allergic to lamb is because most have never eaten it! Remember that food allergies often take one or more years of exposure to a food to develop. If a cat has never eaten lamb, then he can't possibly be allergic to this protein source. However, if he eats lamb regularly, he can certainly develop a sensitivity to it, just as he could if the protein source in his diet were beef, pork, or chicken.

You may want to reconsider before spending extra money on these hypoallergenic diets for a few other reasons as well. Many lamb and rice diets also contain pork, beef, chicken, or egg. Just because a bag of food says "Lamb and Rice" doesn't mean that those are the only ingredients in the food. Often, they are only the main sources of protein, yet the diet contains many other

potentially allergenic protein sources as well. Finally, consider this: If your pet is eating one of these lamb and rice diets that contains other protein sources, and then develops a food allergy, what will you feed it? Lamb and rice has always been a popular diet to feed pets with food sensitivities because most of these pets had never been exposed to lamb before developing the problem. A pet that develops a food sensitivity eating a lamb and rice diet doesn't have many food choices left. Other diets that can be offered should include a protein source the animal has not eaten before, which means you will have to spend a lot of money on diets that contain fish, rabbit, venison, lobster, crab, or shrimp. While lamb and rice diets won't hurt your pet, think twice about paying extra for these special diets that really don't offer any benefit over other premium foods. Save these "hypoallergenic" foods for the pets that really have food sensitivities!

Your doctor may suspect a food sensitivity in your itchy cat if it fails to respond to conventional treatments such as corticosteroids or antihistamines. Signs you may notice in your cat include generalized itchiness, redness, especially on the face, feet, and abdomen, itchiness and redness of the ears, and sometimes itchiness just of the facial area. Food sensitivities are diagnosed by the doctor performing a food elimination trial. The doctor will prescribe either a commercial hypoallergenic diet or he may give you a recipe for you to prepare a diet at home in order to aid in the diagnosis. An elimination trial with a hypoallergenic diet is tried only after other diagnostic tests, such as skin scrapings for mange and fungal cultures for ringworm, have been done to eliminate these more common diseases. The diet should be the only thing your cat eats for at least four and in some cases twelve weeks. If the itching resolves while she is eating the special diet, food sensitivity is the likely cause of her problem. Some cats have a partial resolution of their itching when on a special diet; this indicates that a food ingredient is only partly responsible for the itching, and other tests must be done to determine other causes.

Other tests that are used when diagnosing a food sensitivity include skin tests and RAST or ELISA blood tests. These tests are highly inaccurate and should not be used as the sole determinant. With regard to the RAST or ELISA blood tests, a positive result does not have much meaning. A negative test, however, does imply that the offending food protein is unlikely to be causing the problem.

If a food sensitivity is diagnosed, the doctor may suggest slowly adding new ingredients to the hypoallergenic diet to see if the itching resumes. If it does, then your cat is sensitive to that ingredient. This particular ingredient is taken off the list of things your pet can safely eat. Once all of the sensitive ingredients have been determined, the doctor will work with you to put together a diet your pet can eat without itching.

Since this introduction of various foods takes a lot of time and patience, some doctors will recommend keeping your cat on the hypoallergenic diet used in the feeding trials for the rest of its life.

Internal Parasites

Intestinal parasites, commonly called worms, are very common in kittens. It has been suggested by experts at the Centers for Disease Control that 100 percent of kittens are infected with roundworms or hookworms. Since parasites occur commonly in kittens, it's important for owners to have a thorough understanding of the problem.

The most common parasites that occur in kittens are roundworms, hookworms, tapeworms, giardia, and coccidia. Giardia and coccidia are not worms but rather protozoan organisms. Transmission of all parasites involves direct contact with another infected pet. For kittens, the most common source of infection is the mother cat or a littermate.

Roundworms

Roundworms can cause illness and even death in kittens if a sufficient number of worms are present. The worms take nutrients from the kitten's intestine that would otherwise be used by the kitten for growth. Your kitten might acquire roundworms from his mother through her feces,

through the placenta prior to birth, when nursing, or from its littermates by ingesting a small amount of their fecal material.

Signs of roundworm infection can include a pot-bellied appearance, rough hair coat, diarrhea (occasionally an adult worm, which resembles a piece of spaghetti, is seen in the diarrhea), coughing (due to the immature worms migrating through the lungs), and vomiting (the vomit often contains one or more worms). Many cases of roundworm infections are diagnosed in normal kittens through a microscopic fecal examination, or "stool" test.

The parasites can also cause health problems in humans, who can ingest the infective eggs in the kitten's feces, stool-contaminated soil, or from contaminated hands or objects. While this sounds disgusting, remember that not everyone washes his hands thoroughly after handling a kitten or disposing of its fecal matter. Most commonly, children who don't have good hygiene and who frequently eat dirt are infected. Several things can happen to an infected child:

•••➡ In most cases the infection is asymptomatic, which means there are no signs of illness and the person doesn't even know he is infected.

•••➡ Two distinct diseases can be seen after ingestion of roundworm eggs. The first is visceral larval migrans, where the larvae (immature worms) migrate through various body tissues. Signs of the disease depend upon which tissues are affected, but commonly fever, liver enlargement, and increased white blood cells (specifically the eosinophils, which often increase in parasitic disease) and gamma globulins are seen. In ocular larval migrans, the second syndrome, the eye is involved. Since this syndrome closely resembles a certain type of eye tumor which can occur in children, correct diagnosis is even more important.

Roundworms are easily treated in kittens and cats with the correct type of anthelmintic, or deworming medication, prescribed by your veterinarian. Owners should avoid using over-the-counter dewormers available at pet stores, as these products may not work. Owners who plan to breed their female cats should consult their veterinarians regarding a regular, prophylactic deworming schedule for the mother and kittens.

Hookworms

As with roundworms, kittens become infected with hookworms by eating infective eggs or larvae (found in another pet's stool or vomit), from transfer through the mother's placenta, or through the mother's milk while nursing. Because a single worm can produce 200,000 eggs a day, and most pets can be infected with one to several hundred worms, transmission of this parasite occurs quite easily. Mature cats (over six months old) that might ingest infective eggs or larvae do not develop problems; the eggs or larvae do not develop into adult worms in the intestines but rather encyst in various muscle tissues, as do roundworms. In a female adult cat, pregnancy can activate the cysts, causing the larvae to migrate across the placenta and into the developing kitten. By the fourth postpartum week, most of the larvae have developed into adult worms in the kitten's intestine and now produce eggs to infect the environment.

Hookworms commonly cause anemia in kittens. In fact, this

may be the most common cause of kitten anemia. The disease is most often diagnosed in a routine fecal examination, although it should be highly suspected in any kitten that is lethargic and has pale or white gums.

In humans, hookworms can cause a syndrome similar to the visceral larval migrans condition seen in roundworm infection. Most commonly, hookworms cause a cutaneous larval migrans syndrome. The hookworm larvae enter the skin after direct contact with infected soil (as commonly happens when walking barefoot through the yard, mud, or sand). Typically, a "creeping eruption" pattern develops in the skin, where the larvae are migrating through the skin.

Hookworms are easily treated using drugs similar to those used to treat roundworms. If you plan to breed your female cat, consult your veterinarian regarding a regular, prophylactic deworming schedule for the mother and kittens.

Tapeworms

Tapeworms can occur in kittens, but they are much less common than roundworm and hookworm infections. The most common cause of tapeworm infection is ingestion of infected fleas. Fleas often feed on cat feces. If a cat is passing tapeworm segments containing eggs in the feces, the flea becomes infected with tapeworms. Your kitten then eats the flea and becomes infected.

Tapeworms are easy for owners to diagnose but are often difficult for the doctor to detect. Unlike the other worms, eggs are not laid directly in the feces but rather are contained in the tapeworm segments seen in the feces. The segments resemble grains of rice; when first laid, they are white, about 1/2 inch long, and alive. With time, the segments die and resemble brown rice. Owners who detect tapeworm segments in their pet's feces or on the hair surrounding the anus should contact their veterinarian for the appropriate deworming medication. Humans can only be infected with this type of tapeworm by accidentally ingesting a flea!

Coccidia

Coccidia are microscopic, one-celled protozoan organisms. They are a common cause of diarrhea, which is often bloody, in young kittens. They are transmitted by direct contact with infected feces.

Coccidia are easily diagnosed with a microscopic fecal examination. Treatment involves an appropriate medication for ten days. Owners are not in danger of contracting coccidiosis from their kittens.

Giardia

Like coccidia, giardia are microscopic protozoan organisms. Unlike coccidia, they are often difficult to diagnose. As many as three fecal specimens may need to be examined before the organisms are seen. Many older pets probably harbor the giardia organisms in their intestines without ever showing any signs of illness. As is true with many intestinal parasites, disease is more likely to be seen in and be more severe in kittens. Often the disease is treated despite a negative fecal test if it is suspected. This disease can cause diarrhea, bloating, and gas in kittens. The diarrhea often has a "cow-patty" appearance, is pale and very foul-smelling. Weight loss and poor body condition are also symptoms. Humans can get this disease by direct contact with infective feces; campers are frequently infected by drinking water from streams or ponds where animals eliminate. Giardia

is treated with oral medication, usually metronidazole, prescribed by your veterinarian. Some cases of giardia are not cured with standard doses of metronidazole. Because of this, and because some pets can show signs of toxicity with higher doses of the drug (including vomiting, diarrhea, unsteady gait, and seizures), fenbendazole is another choice. Most small kittens are treated with furazolidone, which is more palatable and easier to administer than the bitter-tasting metronidazole.

Heartworms

It might seem odd to discuss heartworm infection in a book about kittens. After all, the cat is not the natural host for the worm (dogs are). However, cats can get heartworm infection, especially if they spend time outdoors.

Unlike the disease in dogs, cats don't always show the typical signs of coughing, weakness, and weight loss. Some cats with heartworm disease have only chronic vomiting as their clinical sign. There are other differences between dog and cat heartworm disease. Cats usually have fewer adult worms in the heart and lung and usually no baby worms in the blood, which make it more difficult to diagnose.

Also, the treatment is more likely to cause side effects (including death) in cats (the treatment is usually very safe in dogs). Since cats can become infected with heartworms, it's a good idea for kitten owners to have an understanding of this condition.

If the truth be known, heartworms should probably be named lung worms or blood vessel worms. That's because in most cases, the worms actually live in the pulmonary (lung) vessels. Worms are only found in the heart in severe infections, where they start out in the blood vessels of the lungs and "back up" into the heart. However, when heartworms were first discovered most dogs probably had such severe infections that many worms were seen in the heart as well as the pulmonary vessels, and the name heartworm was born.

This disease almost never occurs in young kittens, due to the long life cycle. However, it's important to know about it because your new kitten may need to take medication to prevent this disease from ever occurring.

Heartworms are transmitted by the bite of a mosquito. When a mosquito bites a pet that has heartworms, it transmits some of the microscopic baby worms (called microfilariae) as it feeds on the pet's blood. These microfilariae go through several molts or growing stages in the mosquito's body. After the molts, the mosquito can transmit the disease to the next pet it bites if that pet is not regularly taking a preventive medication.

After the pet acquires the larval heartworms from the mosquito, the larvae spend about six months slowly making their way to the pet's heart and pulmonary vessels. About six months after the mosquito bite, the dog or cat has adult heartworms living in its pulmonary vessels, heart, or both, depending upon the number of worms present.

Since it takes at least six months from the time of the mosquito bite (assuming the mosquito is carrying the baby heartworms) until the first adult heartworms are seen, a dog or cat would need to be at least six months old before it could ever have a heartworm infection.

Heartworm disease is easily diagnosed in dogs with a blood test for heartworms.

In cats, since they have fewer heartworms than dogs, the blood test is not always accurate. Chest radiographs (X-rays), an EKG, and clinical signs are often necessary to diagnose heartworm disease.

Treatment is controversial. Some doctors choose to treat the infection, whereas others choose to just treat any signs the cat may exhibit. Ultimately, the heartworms will die on thier own. Supportive care may be necessary to prevent worsening of the disease in an individual cat. Your veterinarian will review all of your options or refer you to a cardiologist if your cat develops heartworm disease.

External Parasites

Mange

Mange, while a common parasite infection of the skin in puppies and dogs, doesn't occur often in kittens. The parasite is a microscopic insect called a mite.

The most common kind of mange is called notoedric mange, named after the mite that causes the disease. This disease is very itchy. Notoedric mange is also very easily transmitted to other pets and pet owners by close contact with an infected cat or its bedding!

Treatment involves a medicated dip or oral or injectable ivermectin drug therapy. Ivermectin is not approved by the FDA for treating mange; nevertheless, many drugs used in treating pets are not FDA approved but are safe and effective when used properly under veterinary supervision.

Sarcoptic mange usually responds quickly to therapy. However, it is a disease which is easily misdiagnosed, since it resembles other skin diseases, and as many as half of the skin scrapings used to make the diagnosis may not reveal sarcoptic mange mites.

Ear Mites

Ear mites are another form of mange, but most often only the ears are affected. This condition is caused by a mite called *Otodectes cynotis*. The disease is readily transmitted between pets of various species. I have seen several cases in which there was no known exposure to another pet for some time. Rarely, ear mites can be transmitted to owners.

A kitten with ear mites usually will shake its head a lot and scratch its ears. Looking into the ears usually will reveal a large amount of dry, black, crusty exudate resembling dried dirt. The disease is very itchy and the kitten is quite uncomfortable.

The doctor can easily diagnose the infection by looking in the ear with a special instrument called an otoscope (the same thing your doctor uses to look in your ears). The mites are usually seen during the otoscopic exam.

An ear swab needs to be examined microscopically as well, for two reasons. First, occasionally the mites are not seen with the otoscope but they or

---

BACTERIUM, FUNGUS, OR PARASITE............

Kittens are commonly afflicted with skin conditions, or dermatitis. The three most common conditions are pyoderma/folliculitis (caused by bacteria), ringworm (caused by a fungus), and mange (caused by a microscopic parasite called a mite). Unfortunately, all three conditions look alike; certain lab tests must be performed to arrive at a correct diagnosis.

A skin scraping is an easily performed procedure that is used to check for mange mites. There are two types of mange: sarcoptic mange, which can be easily transmitted to owners, and demodectic mange. In some cases of sarcoptic mange, mites won't be found on the skin scraping, so the pet is treated based on the signs of the disease; with demodectic mange, mites are found 99 percent of the time on the scraping, which makes diagnosis easy.

A fungal culture is used to diagnose ringworm. A few hairs and crusts are gently removed from the pet and placed on a special culture plate; if ringworm is the cause of the problem, the fungus usually grows within seven days.

These simple tests make diagnosis and treatment of common kitten skin diseases fairly easy. Rest assured that most cases of kitten dermatitis are not serious and resolve rapidly with prompt treatment.

their eggs are seen microscopically after swabbing the ear. Second, ear mites often cause secondary bacterial or yeast infections that should be treated as well as the mite infection.

Treatment involves a thorough medicated ear flushing to remove the crusty debris. Medicated ear drops can be used; a newer treatment involves using oral or injectable medication, which can be used in conjunction with the drops. Because mites can live outside of the ear canals temporarily, pets treated with ear drops should also be treated with a flea spray to kill the mites. Ear drops should be given for at least one month, which is twice as long as the treatment for other ear diseases; flea spray may also be needed during the course of treatment to

CAT SCRATCH DISEASE. . . . .

Owning a cat is not without some risks. Any cat owner will tell you that cats often scratch, and that's why many people wisely opt to have their cats declawed. Cat bites can cause pasteurella infections in owners; it's important to quickly and thoroughly wash all bites.

Cat scratches can cause a disease called cat scratch disease (also called cat scratch fever). After a cat scratch, the bacteria located on the cat's nails that cause the disease (*Bartonella henselae*) can infect the wound.

Fever and swollen regional lymph nodes occur after the scratch; rarely do more serious signs appear. The disease is diagnosed based on clinical signs and history of exposure to a cat (always tell your doctor you own a cat whenever you develop any illness). A blood test can also be done to confirm the disease.

The disease is often self-limiting and disappears without treatment. Doctors will often prescribe antibiotics and compresses for the swollen lymph nodes.

While cats can carry the bacteria which cause cat scratch disease, cats themselves do not seem to develop disease with this bacteria. Finally, some people with cat scratch disease have no known exposure to a cat, meaning that transmission from the environment or another type of animal has occurred.

kill any mites living outside the ears on the kitten's body. The most common reasons for a pet not to recover from ear mite infections are:

1. Incorrect diagnosis. Treating the ear for mites when in fact the problem could be a bacterial or fungal infection. Microscopic examination of the ear swab will quickly show the difference.

2. Incorrect treatment. Treating the ears for less than one month with the correct ear drops will often result in failure to cure the problem.

Fleas

Depending upon where you live, fleas may or may not be a big problem. If your kitten has fleas, proper flea control is essential. Avoid advice from friends and pet store employees who are not properly trained in flea control. Fleas are a medical problem and as such require a consultation with your doctor, a medical professional who has been trained in parasitology, pharmacology, and toxicology. Every pet owner's situation is different, and there are no flea programs that work on every pet in every situation. Consulting with your veterinarian to develop a flea control

specific to your own unique situation makes sense. Not only that, but he or she probably has a few products that are not available in pet stores. The following information will arm you with the basic facts you need to know about flea control; consult with your doctor for a flea control program customized to your pet's needs.

Proper control requires treating all pets as well as the indoor and outdoor environments, as 95 percent of the flea life cycle occurs **off of the pet and in the environment**.

Prior to starting flea control, thoroughly steam clean your house or apartment at the beginning of the flea season and at the end of the season. This will remove the flea eggs that regular vacuuming won't remove.

1. Begin flea control by vacuuming and mopping the house or apartment.

2. Then, treat *all* pets by bathing and dipping with products recommended by your veterinarian. Bathing and dipping is done every two weeks. Alternatively, using ProSpot plus a Program Flea Control Liquid is preferred for cats and can actually *prevent* fleas when used at the start of the flea season! Use ProSpot every two weeks and *do not dip*

your cat! While ProSpot is not approved for cats, it can be used safely on most cats when used under veterinary supervision. Two new products, Advantage and Frontline, are convenient once-a-month flea products that are great for killing adult fleas and are approved for kittens and cats. They can be used in place of ProSpot.

3. Treat the inside of your house or apartment and the outside (yard) *at the same time* you treat the pets. Your veterinarian may recommend sprays, foggers, borate-based powders (to provide year-round flea control), a professional exterminator, or some combination of these methods. Since 95 percent of the fleas are *off* of the pet and *in* the environment, treating the environment is the *most* important part of the treatment.

4. Use an approved flea spray (applied with a Brushette for maximum effectiveness and minimum waste) or a flea foam (most cats prefer the foam or mousse) on your pet as directed.

5. Flea collars are ineffective by themselves unless used in conjunction with a comprehensive flea program. Electronic collars are also ineffective, as are garlic and brewer's yeast.

6. Repeat as directed by the doctor.

ABOUT FLEA PRODUCTS: Many flea products purchased at stores are ineffective, used incorrectly, or more toxic than products available through your veterinarian. Pet owners who use store-bought products that fail to kill fleas actually end up spending more money than those who start out with the correct products recommended by their veterinarian.

Controlling fleas is not easy or cheap, but by following this information, you should be able to keep your pet relatively free of those irritating little pests.

Fungal Diseases

Ringworm

Ringworm is one of the most common kitten skin diseases. It is not caused by a worm but rather by any of several types of fungi. Ringworm is most commonly caused by transfer of the fungus between pets. However, certain types of ringworm live in the soil and pets (and people) can acquire it through contact with the soil.

Ringworm is so named because the classic skin lesion is a circular, or ring, lesion. It is hairless and often has crusting at the center of the ring and almost always at the periphery of the lesion. Ringworm can occur as just one or a few lesions or can spread and involve the entire body.

Diagnosis is made by culturing affected hairs and some of the scales from the lesion. The culture normally is positive within five to seven days if ringworm is the cause of the disease; some cultures may take two to four weeks for the fungus to grow. If ringworm is suspected, the doctor may begin treatment prior to culture confirmation.

As with many skin diseases, there are several options for treatment. For a few small lesions, often topical treatment with an antifungal medication will work. The generalized form needs more aggressive therapy, including antifungal shampoos and oral medication (which can be expensive). Long-haired animals often need to be thoroughly clipped prior to starting treatment to ensure the best chance

of success. The kitten is treated until it appears "cured" (which may take one or more months of aggressive and expensive treatment), and then for at least two more weeks or until another culture fails to grow ringworm.

Recently a vaccine effective against ringworm has become available. This vaccine can be used as part of the treatment for ringworm and is most effective in situations such as catteries where many cats are exposed to the infection.

Ringworm can be carried asymptomatically (the pet has the ringworm fungus on its body but doesn't show signs of disease), especially by kittens. The ringworm fungus is constantly present in our environment, yet only a few kittens ever show signs of the disease. A suppressed immune system or exposure to a large dose of fungus is often the cause for illness. While ringworm is often passed from pet to owner, too many pets are blamed for causing ringworm in children, when in fact another child is often the culprit. A pet suspected of causing ringworm in a person should always be examined and cultured for the fungus prior to starting expensive treatment.

Miscellaneous Diseases

Intestinal Obstructions

Because kittens are by nature curious, and because like human infants they are prone to chewing on various objects, intestinal obstructions by foreign bodies are more common in kittenhood than at any other time in your cat's life. Any number of objects can be attractive to your kitten and end up in its stomach or intestinal tract. These include play toys, pieces of play toys, small balls, metal objects, jewelry, and string (very common). Rubber and plastic objects are commonly swallowed. These obstructions can be prevented by keeping certain objects, such as jewelry, out of harm's way. Owners should check their kitten's toys as they would a child's to make sure pieces of them (bells, eyes, etc.) are not easily removed. Stuffed animals should not be used as a toy.

Signs of intestinal obstructions are often vague. Vomiting, especially continued vomiting of a projectile or a nonproductive

POISON CONTROL ....

Hopefully you will never need to consult with your doctor about poisoning in your kitten. However, because a kitten is curious and often gets into everything, it may become accidentally poisoned. As with children, prevention is the best cure: don't administer over-the-counter medications without your veterinarian's advice and keep all potential poisons locked up.

If you suspect that your kitten has been poisoned, the best thing you can do is call your veterinarian (or the emergency clinic if after hours) as poisonings are usually true emergencies.

You can also call the National Animal Poison Control Center at 1-800-548-2423 or 1-900-680-0000; both calls cost about $30 and can be used by veterinarians or pet owners. Make sure you keep these numbers, as well as the numbers of your veterinarian and the nearest animal emergency clinic, easily accessible.

nature, can indicate an obstruction. In general, the kitten often doesn't show signs other than vomiting until the condition has persisted for 24 hours or more. This is dangerous; obstructions lasting for several days often cause perforations or rupture of the intestines, which can lead to peritonitis and rapid death. In some kittens, abdominal pain or tenderness can be detected. The veterinarian may even be able to feel the obstruction.

Diagnosis usually requires radiographs (X-rays); in some instances, a barium swallow may be needed to detect rubber toys or partial obstructions. In rare cases, an abdominal exploratory surgery is needed to confirm the suspected obstruction.

Most kittens survive an intestinal obstruction if it is diagnosed early and treated aggressively. Obviously, this is a condition that is better prevented.

Anal Sac Disease

Kittens have two anal sacs located at their anal openings. If you imagine the anus as a clock face, the sacs would be located at approximately the 3 and 9 o'clock positions. These sacs are hidden within tissue that surrounds the anus.

Many people mistakenly refer to the anal sacs as anal glands. Cats do have *anal glands*; however, these are separate and distinct from the anal sacs which often cause problems.

Each anal sac contains glands which produce a foul-smelling liquid secretion. This liquid is stored in the sacs until a bowel movement occurs, at which time the sacs are emptied of their glandular secretion. The function of these anal sac glands is to impart a characteristic odor to the feces, which aids in marking a pet's territory.

Problems arise when the sacs fail to empty. While this is very common in small breeds of dogs, it only occurs rarely in cats. When the sacs don't empty properly, they fill up with the glandular secretions and cause the pet discomfort. Clinical signs seen at this point include the pet scooting its rear end on the ground (in a futile attempt to empty its sacs) or excessive biting and chewing at the rear end (both of these signs can also be seen with tapeworm infections).

If you take your cat to the doctor at this stage, he can simply evacuate the sacs during a digital rectal examination. Since some cats resent this, a sedative or anesthetic may be required. If signs are not seen or are ignored at this stage, the sacs can become impacted and even infected and abscessed. Abscessed anal sacs result when an opening forms in the sacs through the skin; blood and pus ooze from this abscessed area. Treatment for impacted or abscessed sacs is a bit more involved. Often sedation is needed to clean the impacted or abscessed sac. Oral and topical antibiotics are needed to treat the condition as well.

Some pets need to have their anal sacs emptied regularly by the veterinarian. How often your pet will need this done can only be determined by how frequently the sacs fill up.

Chapter 11

Congenital Medical Problems

• •

Congenital conditions are, by definition, any medical problems that are present at birth. They may or may not be hereditary. Even though they may be present at birth, they may not be detected by the owner or veterinarian until the kitten is a bit older (a classic example of this is a heart defect).

Congenital problems occur fairly rarely in cats. Some may be insignificant and not require medical correction, such as small umbilical hernias. Others can be life threatening, such as heart conditions. Most congenital conditions require a diagnosis by a veterinarian; this once again emphasizes the need for frequent veterinary visits and complete physical examinations during the first few months of your kitten's life.

Eye Conditions

• •

Tear Staining

Some breeds of cats, especially Persians and Himalayans, normally have excess tearing. You may notice that the face on either side of the nostrils is wet and the hair, especially light-colored hair, is discolored a brown or copper color. This occurs as a result of a difference in the shape of the skull in these specific

131

breeds of cats. Those with a "pushed-in" face are more likely to have excess tearing as a result of an abnormal lacrimal "lake" in the eyelids (these same breeds often have respiratory problems and/or "noisy" breathing as well). Since the tears don't drain properly, they flow onto the facial skin. Usually no treatment is prescribed other than regular cleaning of the tears and face, although surgical correction may be attempted in more severe cases. Some cats with excess tear production may improve when taking a nutritional supplement called the Missing Link.

Occasionally there is an abnormality of the nasolacrimal ducts, the ducts that normally drain tears from the eyes into the nostrils. Sometimes this occurs when the tear ducts are infected or inflamed, causing them to become clogged with mucus. Occasionally, the tear duct is not normal and can't function properly; surgery may be needed to correct the abnormality or make a new hole for the duct to drain the tears.

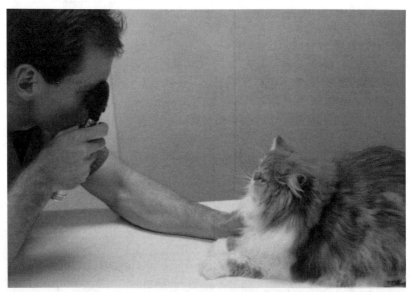

Persian cats normally have excess tearing. No treatment is usually needed other than regular cleaning of the tears and face. Here the doctor performs a thorough ophthalmic examination. Nutritional supplementation can help control the problem. Surgical correction may be attempted in more severe cases.

Heart Conditions

Congenital heart problems rarely occur in kittens. These heart problems are most commonly diagnosed during the physical examination when the doctor listens to the heart and lungs with a stethoscope. Normal heart sounds are described as a "lub-dub;" occasionally, the doctor may hear a heart murmur which sounds like a swooshing sound ("lub-swoosh," "swoosh-lub," or "swoosh-swoosh"). A heart murmur is caused by abnormal, turbulent blood flow through the heart or vessels leading from the heart. Blood flow can become turbulent under several conditions:

1. A blood vessel is narrowed;
2. A hole is present in the wall of the heart;
3. Heart valves are leaky, allowing blood to flow back-ward—out of the heart—instead of forward—through the heart and into the vessels leading to the lungs (pulmonary artery) or body (aorta).

Sometimes, the doctor may hear an "innocent" murmur. This is a soft murmur that usually disappears by four to six months of age and is not a sign of heart disease.

Depending upon the loudness (intensity) and location of the murmur, the doctor will usually have some idea what type of congenital heart problem exists. Additional testing (chest X-rays, an ultrasound examination of the heart) may be required to define the exact type of congenital heart defect. Depending upon the cause of the problem, heart surgery may be required if the defect is severe.

Miscellaneous Congenital Conditions

Umbilical Hernia

A hernia is a hole in the body wall; an umbilical hernia is a hole in the umbilical (belly button) area. Umbilical hernias are most often congenital; while the hole is present at birth, the herniation (material sticking through the hole) may not develop until later in life. Since umbilical hernias can be hereditary, affected cats should not be bred.

Most kittens with umbilical hernias have small hernias with only a small amount of abdominal fat sticking through the hole. Very small hernias usually cause no problems and don't have to be corrected, although they often are when the pet is spayed or neutered. Larger hernias should always be corrected. If not corrected surgically, there is a chance other tissues such as intestines could become entrapped in the hernia. Also, any trauma the kitten might experience later in life (such as a fall or if accidentally struck by a car) could enlarge the hernia even more, causing serious problems.

Cryptorchidism/ Monorchidism

By birth, the testicles of most male kittens have descended into the scrotum, although they are so small they may be difficult to detect in many kittens. Usually, this happens shortly after birth or within a few weeks of birth. Sometimes, something goes wrong and one or both testicles fail to descend into the scrotum. If both testicles fail to descend, the condition is called cryptor-

chidism and the kitten is a cryptorchid. Far more common is the condition in which one testicle descends but the other does not; in this situation, called monorchidism, the kitten is a monorchid.

Testicles need to be located in the scrotum or the retained testicle is infertile. However, retained testicles still produce the male hormone testosterone beginning at puberty. Retained testicles have a much higher incidence of cancer than scrotal testicles; all animals with one or both testicles that are retained need to be neutered. The hidden testicle is often located in the abdomen, but occasionally it is located just underneath the skin in front of the scrotum (the inguinal or groin area). Since the retained testicle can be located anywhere in the abdominal cavity, the surgery to remove it combines a normal neutering for the scrotal testicle and exploratory surgery to remove the retained one. Monorchid cats should not be used for breeding as they can pass this condition on to their male offspring; it is also considered unethical to breed monorchid cats. Cryptorchid cats, being infertile, cannot father offspring.

Chapter 12

Lifeplan

• •

One of the most important things veterinarians can do for their clients is inform them what medical care their pet will need throughout its life and the associated costs. While this book focuses on kittens, this chapter is about adult cats as well as kittens. In the next few pages you will find a description of the care your kitten will need as it grows into adulthood, mid-life, and its golden years as a geriatric pet. By knowing what care your kitten will need throughout its life, you can better plan ahead.

Two Months Old (8 Weeks)

First veterinary visit (although this can also occur at 6 weeks of age if you acquire the kitten then):

••➡ Complete physical examination

••➡ First kitten vaccinations: Feline Viral Rhinotracheitis-Calici Virus-Panleukopenia-Chlamydia (FVRCP) (Note: Not all veterinarians vaccinate against the respiratory infection caused by the chlamydia organism)

••➡ Fecal exam for intestinal parasites

••➡ Heartworm preventive medication may be started on the kitten's first visit, depending upon the area of the country where you live and if the kitten will be an outdoor pet. I personally recommend keeping pets indoors to decrease the chance of illness, injury, or fatalities. Heartworm disease, while it can occur in cats, occurs much less often than dogs. Prescribing heartworm preventive medication is controversial; the medicine, while safe to use in cats as pre-

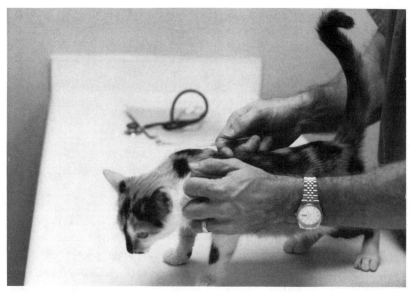

Your kitten requires a series of vaccinations throughout its lifetime.

scribed by your veterinarian, is not approved for use in cats. Since the disease is difficult to diagnose in cats, expensive to treat, and since the treatment has more side effects in cats than in dogs, I recommend that cats that spend any time outdoors be placed on heartworm preventive medication. Check with your doctor to see if your cat would benefit from heartworm preventive medication.

Three Months Old (12 Weeks)

Second veterinary visit:

•• ➡ Complete physical examination

•• ➡ Second kitten vaccinations: Feline Viral Rhinotracheitis-Calici Virus-Panleukopenia-Chlamydia (FVRCP) (Note: Not all veterinarians vaccinate against the respiratory infection caused by the chlamydia organism.)

•• ➡ Feline Leukemia/Feline Immunodeficiency Virus (FIV) Test (also called the Feline AIDS test)

•• ➡ First Feline Leukemia Vaccination

The leukemia/FIV test determines if your young kitten is infected with either of these fatal viruses. If the tests are negative, your kitten can receive its leukemia vaccination (there is not currently a vaccine for FIV, or feline AIDS infection). Kittens that test positive on either test should be retested in four to eight weeks. If the second test is negative, either the kitten eliminated the virus, the first test gave a "false-positive" reaction, or the virus is "hidden" in the kitten's body and will cause problems later. If the second series of tests is negative, the kitten can be vaccinated against leukemia.

Some doctors recommend vaccinating against feline infectious peritonitis (FIP), a contagious fatal disease which usually affects young outdoor cats. Because this vaccine is new and the subject of some controversy, not all doctors recommend it. You should discuss FIP with your doctor if you have any questions.

Four Months Old (16 Weeks)

Third veterinary visit:

• • ➡ Complete physical examination

• • ➡ Third kitten vaccinations: Feline Viral Rhinotracheitis-Calici Virus-Panleukopenia-Chlamydia (FVRCP) (Note: Not all veterinarians vaccinate against the respiratory infection caused by the chlamydia organism)

• • ➡ Second Feline Leukemia Vaccination

• • ➡ Rabies Vaccination (this may be given during the second visit depending upon local laws)

• • ➡ Fecal exam for intestinal parasites

The estimated cost for the first three kitten visits is approximately $150.

Four To Six Months Old

• • ➡ Spaying or neutering

• • ➡ Declawing

• • ➡ Tattooing/Microchipping

Tattooing and microchipping serve as permanent forms of identification in the event that the pet is lost or stolen (some estimates are that one in four cats will become "lost" at some point in their lives). Tattooing and microchipping are painless and are usually performed when the kitten is spayed or neutered for convenience. The tattoo, an identification number, is usually placed on the inside of either hind leg; the microchip is implanted under the skin in the shoulder area. More important than the tattoo and microchip is the registry; make sure the tattoo and microchip are registered with a national pet registry.

The estimated cost for the spaying or neutering and tattooing and microchipping will vary with the size of the pet at the time of surgery. The cost is approximately $225 for female kittens undergoing the tattooing, microchipping, ovariohysterectomy (spay), and declawing surgeries, and approximately $185 for male cats undergoing the tattooing, microchipping, neutering, and declawing procedures.

Twelve Months Old

At 12 months of age, your kitten is now an adult cat.

At 12 months of age, your kitten will go for its one-year visit. During the visit, the doctor will perform a thorough examination of your now adult cat. Your veterinarian will discuss important

health and wellness information with you at this visit such as the following:

• •➡ The kitten should be switched to an adult maintenance diet. Adult cats can have food left down all day, as long as they are used to this type of feeding and do not become obese. You can feed your cat once or twice daily as another option. Obese pets will be started on a medically controlled diet. Many owners ask about dry versus wet food. While cats prefer wet food, they don't need it. As a compromise, many owners feed a small amount of wet food once or twice daily and leave dry food available at all times for the cat to eat as it desires.

TRAVELING IN THE CAR ....

It is important that your kitten travel well in the car. While most owners don't take their pets everywhere with them, they need to be comfortable enough so that the trip to the veterinarian is pleasant.

Start by taking your kitten on frequent short trips in the car. Getting your kitten used to short trips at an early age will prevent future "car sickness" and will make traveling easier. To prevent the fear of traveling that many pets have, be sure to take them in the car to places *other* than just the doctor's office, such as the park. If the kitten associates the car with a fun, pleasant experience at an early age, it shouldn't have any trouble riding in the car when it is older.

••➡ Continue daily vitamins. Many doctors start kittens on Prozyme, an enzyme supplement, to aid in digestion and absorption of nutrients; decrease food intake by 10 to 20 percent after one month if your cat gains weight. Continue the Prozyme for the life of your pet to maximize nutrient absorption from its diet. Prozyme may also help your pet's coat look better and decrease excess shedding.

••➡ The next set of vaccinations, fecal test for parasites, and physical examination occurs in four months (at sixteen months of age) and annually thereafter.

The baseline blood profile will also be done at this time. The purpose of this blood profile is to find out what is normal for your pet. While normal values are established and published in veterinary books, your pet may have a value outside the normal range yet not have any diseases. Establishing what is normal for your pet will help when your pet gets sick and a blood profile, done at the time of illness, can be compared with the normal, baseline profile.

••➡ Cats that have not been spayed or neutered need that done now. Early (four to six

---

FEAR OF FLYING. . . . .

Occasionally an owner wants to take a kitten on the plane for a trip. Each airline has its own requirements and should be contacted *at least* one month prior to traveling. Following are a few general tips that can make the trip go smoother for you and your kitten:

1. Most airlines require a health certificate from the veterinarian stating the kitten is healthy enough to fly. Generally, the certificate should be obtained within ten days of the trip.

2. Many pets do better when sedated. Your doctor can discuss sedation with you. Because no two pets require the same dose of medicine nor act the same when on the drug, you might consider a trial dose a few days before the trip to make sure you get the desired effect (mild sedation).

3. Kittens can usually travel in a carrier under your seat if the carrier fits comfortably there. Otherwise, they travel in the cargo hull of the plane, which is pressurized for comfort.

months of age) spaying and neutering can prevent medical problems (such as breast cancer in female cats) and behavioral problems. Most pets have been spayed or neutered by one year of age. Some owners may put it off thinking they want to breed their pets but then change their minds. No matter how old your pet is, it's never to late to have the surgery done!

•••➡ If you plan to breed your cat, the ideal time is usually between two and five years of age (especially for females).

•••➡ The first oral surgery (ultrasonic dental scaling) for dental disease is performed at two to three years of age, and annually thereafter. Dental disease is the most common disease in cats; early diagnosis, treatment, and home care are critical to saving your pet's teeth, gums, and jaws, and preventing the spread of harmful oral bacteria throughout the body.

•••➡ At eight years of age, cats are considered "mid-life" pets. They need a mini-blood profile and often a urinalysis at least every one to two years until twelve years of age. The results of this blood test will be compared to the initial baseline

profile done when the pet was vaccinated at sixteen months of age. Any changes may indicate early kidney or liver disease, diabetes, or cancer.

•••➡ At twelve years of age, cats need a complete blood profile annually. As costs allow, they should also get a urinalysis, EKG, and chest radiographs (X-rays) annually to look for signs of kidney, liver, and heart disease, and cancer, which are more common in older pets. Early diagnosis prevents pain and suffering and is less expensive than treatment of an ill or dying pet.

This lifeplan is advised for all cats, although your own veterinarian's recommendations may differ slightly. Regular veterinary visits and laboratory testing are needed to prevent serious disease. As with humans, preventing disease is preferred to treating a disease; it is also much less expensive.

The annual cost of veterinary care obviously will differ depending upon the needs of your own specific pet. For example, while most pets need their first oral surgery for periodontal disease at two to three years of age, some cats build up tartar (infection) much slower. They may not need the surgery until four to five years of age. Their care would be less expensive than that of a pet that requires annual ultrasonic scalings starting at two years of age.

For the typical cat that requires two veterinary visits a year (one for its annual vaccinations and examination, one visit for a minor illness) and a dental ultrasonic scaling each year, the approximate cost would be $175. This does not include major illnesses, food, grooming, boarding, toys, or treats. While $175 may seem like a lot, realize that you do not normally spend this on one visit but rather over the course of a year. Also keep in mind that this amounts to a little more than fifty cents per day, which is not much to spend on the pet you love.

Recent surveys indicate the average cat owner is willing to spend approximately $550 per year on his pet.

When It's Time to Say Goodbye

At some point in your pet's life, you may be faced with the difficult decision to euthanize your cat. Usually, the pet is older and has been ill for some time. In some cases, a kitten must be euthanized for medical or financial reasons.

Most veterinarians do not like the term "putting the pet to sleep." The pet is not going to sleep; it is being killed, its life is ending. Young children who hear the term "put to sleep" may be shocked when the pet doesn't wake up. Some are terrified that when they go to sleep they will end up like the pet and not wake up. Be honest with your children. While euthanasia is difficult for all involved, it is an opportune time to explain death and dying to young children and help them come to accept this natural part of living.

The process of euthanasia, while a painful decision for owners, is a simple one. Most of the time the process involves a painless intravenous injection of an overdose of an anesthetic agent. The pet quickly and quietly becomes unconscious, breathing ceases, and the heart stops beating within a minute or two.

Owners often inquire about being present during the procedure. Most doctors are not opposed to this, but you should carefully consider whether this is truly what you want. Many owners don't want to see their pet dead and would rather remember the good times they had with their pet. For others, being present when the pet dies is comforting to them and their pet and helps them with the grieving process. If you choose to be present, here are a few things to remember:

••➡ The procedure is painless; the only thing your pet feels is the needle being introduced into the vein, similar to when it gets a shot or has blood drawn.

••➡ Pets pick up on your emotions. While it may be hard to contain your emotions during the procedure, the pet will be more comfortable if you can postpone grieving until the procedure is completed and the pet is dead.

••➡ Rarely, some pets may make sounds during the procedure, exhibit muscle twitching after the procedure, or eliminate feces or urine. These are rare occurrences but can be discomforting to owners. Rest assured

that if these events occur, they occur *after* death; the pet is totally unaware of them, has no voluntary control of these functions, and feels no pain.

After euthanasia, the pet's body must be disposed of. Several options are available:

••➡ Some owners choose to take the pet home and bury it in the yard. While many cities have laws prohibiting this, it is unlikely your doctor would turn you in for choosing this option. If you choose home burial, remember to bury the pet several feet underground in a container so that other animals or pets cannot dig up the body.

••➡ The other option, more commonly selected, involves the hospital disposing of the pet. This may be done through the city's animal control office or a pet cemetery, which cremates the body and disposes of the ashes. Owners can also choose a more elaborate option such as private cremation, where the ashes are returned to you in an urn for private burial in a grave.

Chapter 13

Lowering the Cost of Pet Care

• •

Everyone, including doctors, agrees that the cost of medical care is high. Even medical care for our furry friends can be expensive at times. While every owner would like to get the best care for his pet at the lowest price, going to the "lowest bidder" for pet health care can be a mistake!

As an owner, you and you alone will have to decide whether low cost or high quality is more important. If you choose higher-quality care, there are still things you can do to lower the cost of health care and not sacrifice quality or service. Keep in mind that the average cost of health care for a 10-pound cat (excluding major illnesses) is about $200 per year. While

studies show that the average pet owner is willing to spend approximately $550 per year on a pet, the following suggestions will help you cut that cost without sacrificing quality of care.

1. Have your cat examined and vaccinated at least annually. Annual examinations and vaccinations are the least expensive way to prevent diseases that can easily cause severe illness and in some cases kill your pet. A cat can be fully protected against the major communicable diseases for under $100 a year. And where should you take your pet for these vaccinations? As a rule, it's no more expensive (and in some cases it's less expensive) to go to a full-service animal hospital than a low-cost vaccination clinic.

2. Some cats should receive heartworm preventative medication. The cost for heartworm treatment is about $500, and heartworm treatment is associated with more serious side effects in cats than in dogs. For a fraction of the cost you can prevent this deadly disease. Most doctors prescribe heartworm preventative medication for cats that spend a portion of their time outdoors, but check with your doctor to see if your cat would benefit from taking the monthly heartworm medicine.

3. Practice preventive medicine. Common sense tells us it's cheaper to prevent something than fix it. Disease prevention costs little compared to the cost of treating a sick pet. Periodontal disease is the most common disease in pets. Regular dental cleanings will prevent more serious problems (abscesses, sinus infections, etc.). Since the incidence of expensive and serious diseases increases as our pets age, annual geriatric examinations and blood and urine tests for our older pets are needed to allow early disease detection.

4. Get pet health insurance. No pet should be euthanized because an owner can't afford medical care. Pet health insurance is extremely inexpensive and allows owners the opportunity to have expensive procedures such as cancer chemotherapy performed when the alternative might be death for the pet.

5. Open a savings account for your pet. You don't want to pay for health insurance? Open a bank account for your pet instead. At $1 per day, funding this account for just five years will create a nest egg for "pet emergencies" of $1,825 (not including interest). If you think this idea sounds silly, consider this: the money in the account is more than most owners will ever need to spend for emergency care for their pets. When your pet dies at the ripe old age of 15-20 years old, close the account and spend the balance on yourself! If nothing else you are saving money for something; if your pet doesn't need it, you have a nice little nest egg to enjoy.

6. Ask your doctor about ways to cut health care costs. Many doctors offer money-saving programs while not cutting the quality of care. For example, some doctors offer referral incentive programs. For each new client you refer, both your friend and you save 10 percent on your next visits. This can allow you to save a little on every visit; the more new friends you refer, the more you save!

Other doctors offer multi-pet discounts: if you own two or more pets and have them vaccinated at the same time, your bill is discounted based on the number of pets.

Another cost-cutting idea we developed for our clients is a VIP, or Very Important Pet, program. Each time you visit, your total bill is recorded on a VIP card. When you fill up your card, you receive credit on your next visit for the average amount you spent on prior visits. This allows

you substantial savings, yet you receive excellent medical care.

Some doctors offer monthly specials. For example, since February is Pet Dental Health Month, some hospitals offer a reduced price on teeth cleanings during that month. This allows you to save a little money on a much-needed service.

Saving money is important to everyone. Veterinary medicine can offer advanced diagnostic tests and treatments for many serious diseases; however, these can be expensive. Cutting costs of health care can be done without compromising care. Considering the suggestions in this chapter will allow you to offer your pet high-quality care at an affordable price.

Chapter 14

Common Kitten Breeds

● ●

Most owners purchase alley cats or the popular domestic short hair (DSH) or domestic long hair (DLH) cats. However, some owners favor a specific breed of cats. If you decide to purchase a purebred cat, there are many breeds from which to choose. This chapter lists some of the attributes of some of the most popular breeds. If your breed isn't listed, I encourage

American short hair cat

you to visit with your veterinarian or attend a local cat show. Learn everything you can about the breed of kitten you wish to purchase before making your buying decision. One word of warning: pure breeds usually have more medical problems than mixed breeds. Don't be discouraged by the number of possible problems listed in this chapter. Any pet can become ill, and just because a certain breed has specific problems common to that breed, doesn't mean your new kitten will necessarily develop those problems.

SIAMESE

This popular breed of cat comes in several varieties or color points: the seal point which has dark brown or black points, the blue point which has blue points with a gray body, the lilac point which has pink-gray points and a white body, and the chocolate point which has chocolate-colored points and a pale ivory body. By points, we are referring to the ears, legs, feet, and face (mask). The Siamese cat has beautiful blue eyes.

All kittens are born light and darken with age. The pigment

Siamese cat

darkens where the temperature is lower, and older cats generally are darker than younger ones.

The Siamese most people are familiar with have a rounded face. However, the true Siamese has a sleek and slender body and a long, narrow face.

Most cats are energetic and affectionate. The Siamese is very vocal and has a distinctive voice which some owners find irritating (especially when the females come into heat). Wool sucking, the desire to suck on certain types of clothing, is a behavioral problem that can be seen in Siamese cats.

Strabismus, or cross-eyes, is a normal condition seen in Siamese that develops shortly after birth. It is an actual defect in the ocular pathway in the brain, and Siamese cats have a more narrow range of vision than other cats due to this problem.

Dental disease, including cervical erosions (similar to cavities in people) occurs in many cats but especially in Siamese cats. Regular (every six to twelve months) dental cleanings done under anesthesia by the veterinarian will help control the condition.

Common Problems
Acromegaly, symmetrical alopecia, vitiligo, hyperesthesia syndrome, adenocarcinoma of the intestine, malignant breast cancer, gangliosidosis, mucopolysaccharidosis, congenital heart disease, sphingomyelinosis, hydrocephalus, bronchial disease, hypotrichosis, psychogenic alopecia, esophageal hypomotility, glaucoma, hip dysplasia.

HIMALAYAN

The Himalayan is a cross between the Siamese and the Persian. These cats resemble Persians and exhibit color variations of their points. As with the Siamese, the eyes are blue. Due to the long coat, daily grooming is a necessity. Himalayans are generally gentle cats that are calm and quiet and make good lap cats.

Common Problems
Cataracts, psychogenic alopecia, cutaneous asthenia, polycystic kidney disease, neonatal isoerythrolysis.

PERSIAN

The Persian is one of the most popular breeds of cat. They are gentle and require daily brushing due to their long coat. Mats in the coat and hairballs are often encountered in these cats. There are six color types for the breed and each type or division contains many points. The six divisions are the solid division, shaded, tabby, smoke, particolor, and Himalayan or pointed division. The eyes are blue.

Common Problems

Eyelid problems (entropion), excessive tearing from the eyes (epiphora), glaucoma, skin fold dermatitis, bladder stones (urnary calculi), seforrhea, studtail, stenoticnares (small nasal openings), polycystic kidney disease, patellar luxation (dislocating knee caps), neonatal isoerythrolysis (a fatal blood disorder causing fading kitten syndrome), and hip dysplasia.

REX

There are two varieties of the rex, the Devon Rex and the Cornish Rex. While closely related, there are differences in the genetics of these two cats. The Devon Rex has a wavy coat, whereas the Cornish Rex has a curly coat. Both rexes have soft coats of fine hair; those who are allergic

Persian cat

to cat hair might consider these cats. Each rex has several recognized color patterns.

Common Problems

Hypotrichosis, hypothyroidism, neonatal isoerythrolysis, patellar subluxation, hip dysplasia, and spasticity.

MAINE COON

The Maine Coon is one of the oldest breeds in America. Many color patterns are recorded, although the brown tabby is most popular. These cats are generally large and strong and have a heavy coat. The long coat requires daily brushing. Maine Coons are usually affectionate animals which enjoy companionship.

Common Problems

Few problems are recognized in this breed. Pectus excavatum, patellar luxation, and hip dysplasia.

SCOTTISH FOLD

This breed, which originated in Scotland in the early 1960s, has a curved or lop ear. The gene responsible for this trait expresses incomplete dominance, which means that the gene must be present in at least one parent in order to pass the trait on to the kittens. Occasionally, straight-eared kittens are produced. Kittens are born with normal ears that become curved by one month of age. Scottish Folds are sweet cats with soft voices that enjoy affection from owners. Unlike the vocal Siamese, Scottish Folds are fairly quiet cats.

Common Problems

Ear infections (including ear mites) and neonatal isoerythrolysis.

MANX

The Manx, from the Isle of Man, is the "tailless" cat. The tailless feature is the result of a mutated dominant gene (the Manx gene). In addition to missing a tail, the Manx is unique in that it has a round face, a short back, and front legs which are usually smaller than the rear legs. Some Manx will have vestiges of a tail and a few will actually possess a full tail.

Common Problems

Spina bifida, atresia ani, rectal prolapse, corneal dystrophy, and pyoderma.

RUSSIAN BLUE

The Russian Blue is a beautiful cat that has a blue or blue-gray coat. The eyes are a startling green color. The short coat should be brushed; these cats shed less than other breeds and are very clean.

Common Problems

There are no obvious recognized problems unique to this breed.

RAGDOLL/SNOWSHOE

The Ragdoll is a beautiful long-haired cat. While it appears to be a long-haired Snowshoe, that is not technically true. It developed as a cross between a Persian and a Birman. The cat will usually relax when held, and that is how it came to be called a Ragdoll.

The Snowshoe is a beautiful short-haired cat. The breed was developed by crossing the white markings of an American Shorthair with a Siamese. The cat gets its name from the white markings on its feet.

Both breeds make good pets and enjoy affection from owners.

Common Problems

There are no specific medical problems recognized in the Ragdoll or Snowshoe.

Index

A
Abscess, 33
Acne, 106
Additives (food), 59
Advil, 41
Aggression, 6
AIDS, cat, 104-105, 136-137
Allergy, food, 110-115
Anal glands, 128
Anal sacs, 128-129
Anesthesia, 80-83
Antibodies, 28-32
Antidiarrheals, 41
Antigen, 28, 33
Antigenic, 111
Antihistamines, 44, 109-110
Aspirin, 41, 98
Association of American Feed
    Control Officials, 55, 57, 62
Atopic dermatitis, 110
Atopy/Allergies, 107-110

B
Bathing, 39
Behavior, 82, 89-94
Benadryl, 44
Boarding, 7, 24-25
Breeding, 75-87
Brushing, 2, 43, 67, 71, 73-74

Brushing teeth, 9

C
Calories, 50
Carbohydrates, 50
Cardiomyopathy, 95-99
    dilated, 96
    hypertrophic, 96
Castration complex, 79
Cat breeds, specific:
    Himalayan, 2, 131, 149-150
    Maine Coon, 151
    Manx, 151
    Persian, 2, 131, 150
    Ragdoll/Snowshoe, 152
    Rex, 2, 150-151
    Russian Blue, 152
    Siamese, 2, 148-149
    Scottish Fold, 151
Cat Scratch Disease, 123
Clipper burn, 74
Coccidia, 118-119
Congenital diseases, 131-134
    cryptorchidism, 134
    heart conditions, 135
    monorchidism, 134
    tear staining, 131-132
    umbilical hernia, 133-134
Corticosteroids, 42-43, 109

Other Books from Republic of Texas Press

100 Days in Texas: The Alamo Letters
by Wallace O. Chariton
Alamo Movies
by Frank Thompson
At Least 1836 Things You Ought to Know About Texas but Probably Don't
by Doris L. Miller
Civil War Recollections of James Lemuel Clark and the Great Hanging at Gainesville, Texas in October 1862
by L.D. Clark
Cow Pasture Pool: Golf on the Muni-tour
by Joe E. Winter
A Cowboy of the Pecos
by Patrick Dearen
Cripple Creek Bonanza
by Chet Cunningham
Daughter of Fortune: The Bettie Brown Story
by Sherrie S. McLeRoy
Defense of a Legend: Crockett and the de la Peña Diary
by Bill Groneman
Don't Throw Feathers at Chickens: A Collection of Texas Political Humor
by Charles Herring Jr. and Walter Richter
Eight Bright Candles: Courageous Women of Mexico
by Doris E. Perlin
Etta Place: Her Life and Times with Butch Cassidy and the Sundance Kid
by Gail Drago
Exiled: The Tigua Indians of Ysleta del Sur
by Randy Lee Eickhoff
Exploring Dallas with Children: A Guide for Family Activities
by Kay McCasland Threadgill
Exploring the Alamo Legends
by Wallace O. Chariton
Eyewitness to the Alamo
by Bill Groneman
From an Outhouse to the White House
by Wallace O. Chariton

The Funny Side of Texas
by Ellis Posey and John Johnson
Ghosts Along the Texas Coast
by Docia Schultz Williams
The Great Texas Airship Mystery
by Wallace O. Chariton
Henry Ossian Flipper, West Point's First Black Graduate
by Jane Eppinga
Horses and Horse Sense: The Practical Science of Horse Husbandry
by James "Doc" Blakely
How the Cimarron River Got Its Name and Other Stories About Coffee
by Ernestine Sewell Linck
The Last Great Days of Radio
by Lynn Woolley
Letters Home: A Soldier's Legacy
by Roger L. Shaffer
More Wild Camp Tales
by Mike Blakely
Noble Brutes: Camels on the American Frontier
by Eva Jolene Boyd
Outlaws in Petticoats and Other Notorious Texas Women
by Gail Drago and Ann Ruff
Phantoms of the Plains: Tales of West Texas Ghosts
by Docia Schultz Williams
Rainy Days in Texas Funbook
by Wallace O. Chariton
Red River Women
by Sherrie S. McLeRoy
Santa Fe Trail
by James A. Crutchfield
Slitherin' 'Round Texas
by Jim Dunlap
Spindletop Unwound
by Roger L. Shaffer
Spirits of San Antonio and South Texas
by Docia Schultz Williams and Reneta Byrne
Star Film Ranch: Texas' First Picture Show
by Frank Thompson
Tales of the Guadalupe Mountains
by W.C. Jameson

Call Wordware Publishing, Inc. for names of the
bookstores in your area: (972) 423-0090

Texas Highway Humor
by Wallace O. Chariton
Texas Politics in My Rearview
Mirror
by Waggoner Carr and Byron Varner
Texas Ranger Tales
by Mike Cox
Texas Tales Your Teacher Never
Told You
by Charles F. Eckhardt
Texas Wit and Wisdom
by Wallace O. Chariton
That Cat Won't Flush
by Wallace O. Chariton
That Old Overland Stagecoaching
by Eva Jolene Boyd
This Dog'll Hunt
by Wallace O. Chariton
To The Tyrants Never Yield: A
Texas Civil War Sampler
by Kevin R. Young

Tragedy at Taos: The Revolt of
1847
by James A. Crutchfield
A Trail Rider's Guide to Texas
by Mary Elizabeth Sue Goldman
A Treasury of Texas Trivia
by Bill Cannon
Unsolved Texas Mysteries
by Wallace O. Chariton
Wagon Tongues and the North
Star: Tales of the Cattle Trails
by Eva Jolene Boyd
Western Horse Tales
Edited by Don Worcester
When Darkness Falls: Tales of San
Antonio Ghosts and Hauntings
by Docia Schultz Williams
Wild Camp Tales
by Mike Blakely

Seaside Press

The Bible for Busy People
Book 1: The Old Testament
by Mark Berrier Sr.
Critter Chronicles
by Jim Dunlap
Dallas Uncovered
by Larenda Lyles Roberts
Dirty Dining: A Cookbook, and
More, for Lovers
by Ginnie Siena Bivona
Exotic Pets: A Veterinary Guide
for Owners
by Shawn Messonnier, D.V.M.
I Never Wanted to Set the World
on Fire, but Now That I'm 50,
Maybe It's a Good Idea
by Bob Basso, Ph.D.
Jackson Hole Uncovered
by Sierra Sterling Adare
Just Passing Through
by Beth Beggs
Lives and Works of the Apostles
by Russell A. Stultz
Los Angeles Uncovered
by Frank Thompson
Only: The Last Dinosaur
by Jim Dunlap

Pete the Python: The Further
Adventures of Mark and Deke
by Jim Dunlap
Salt Lake City Uncovered
by Sierra Adare and Candy Moulton
San Antonio Uncovered
by Mark Louis Rybczyk
San Francisco Uncovered
by Larenda Lyles Roberts
Seattle Uncovered
by JoAnn Roe
A Sure Reward
by B.J. Smagula
Survival Kit for Today's Family
by Bill R. Swetmon
They Don't Have to Die (2nd Ed.)
by Jim Dunlap
Tucson Uncovered
by John and Donna Kamper
Twin Cities Uncovered
by The Arthurs
Unlocking Mysteries of God's
Word
by Bill Swetmon
Your Kittens' First Year
by Shawn Messonnier, D.V.M.
Your Puppy's First Year
by Shawn Messonnier, D.V.M.

Call Wordware Publishing, Inc. for names of the
bookstores in your area: (972) 423-0090

Other Books from Wordware Publishing, Inc.

Popular Applications Series
Build Your Own Computer (2nd Ed.)
Creating Help for Windows App.
Developing Utilities in Assembly
  Language
Developing Utilities in Visual
  Basic 4.0
Getting the Most From Your HP
  LaserJet
HP LaserJet Handbook
Learn ACT 3.0 for Win 95 in a Day
Learn AmiPro in a Day (Ver 2.0 &
  3.0)
Learn AutoCAD in a Day
Learn AutoCAD 12 in a Day
Learn AutoCAD LT for Windows
  in a Day
Learn AutoCAD LT for Windows
  95 in a Day
Learn AutoCAD LT Rel. 2 for
  Windows in a Day
Learn C in Three Days
Learn CompuServe for Windows
  in a Day
Learn dBASE Programming in a
  Day (2nd Ed.)
Learn DOS 6.2 in a Day
Learn Generic CADD 6.0 in a Day
Learn Lotus 1-2-3 Rel. 4 for DOS
  in a Day
Learn Lotus 1-2-3 Rel. 4 for
  Windows in a Day
Learn Lotus 1-2-3 Rel. 5 for
  Windows in a Day
Learn MS Access 2.0 for
  Windows in a Day
Learn MS Access 7.0 for Windows
  95 in a Day
Learn Microsoft Assembler in a Day
Learn MS Excel 7.0 for Windows
  95 in a Day
Learn MS PowerPoint 7.0 for
  Windows 95 in a Day
Learn MS Publisher 2.0 for
  Windows in a Day
Learn MS Word 6.0 for Windows
  in a Day

Popular Applications Series (Cont.)
Learn MS Word 7.0 for Windows
  95 in a Day
Learn Microsoft Works in a Day
  (Ver 2.0)
Learn Microsoft Works 3.0 in a Day
Learn Microsoft Works 3.0 for
  Windows in a Day
Learn Novell NetWare Software
  in a Day
Learn PageMaker 5.0 in a Day
Learn PAL 4.5 in a Day
Learn Pascal in Three Days
Learn PROCOMM PLUS 2.0 for
  Widows in a Day
Learn Quattro Pro 5.0 in a Day
Learn to Use Your Modem in a Day
Learn Turbo Assembler in a Day
Learn Visual Basic 4.0 in 3 Days
Learn Visual dBASE 5.5 for
  Windows in a Day
Learn Windows in a Day
Learn Windows 95 in a Day
Learn WordPerfect 5.1+ in a Day
Learn WordPerfect 5.2 for
  Windows in a Day
Learn WordPerfect 6.0 for
  Windows in a Day
Learn WordPerfect Presentations
  in a Day
Moving from WordPerfect for
  DOS to WordPerfect for
  Windows
Networks for Small Businesses
Repair and Upgrade Your Own PC
  (2nd Ed.)
Write TSRs Now
Write Your Own Programming
  Language Using C++ (2nd Ed.)

Programmer's Example Series
The Delphi Programmer's
  Example Book
The WordBasic Example Book
The Visual Basic 4.0 Example Bk
The Visual Basic 97 Example Bk

Call Wordware Publishing, Inc. for names of the
bookstores in your area: (972) 423-0090

Other Books from Wordware Publishing, Inc.

Call Wordware Publishing, Inc. for names of the
bookstores in your area: (972) 423-0090